Be a cool calculator this summer with CGP!

Thirsty for summer Maths practice? This Daily Practice Book from CGP is more refreshing than an orange ice-lolly during a heatwave...

Inside, you'll find a page of Maths practice for every school day of the summer term, covering a huge range of skills from the Year 5 curriculum.

It's perfect for use in class or at home, with plenty of examples and some colourful fun to make sure pupils stay chilled!

What CGP is all about

Our sole aim here at CGP is to produce the highest quality books — carefully written, immaculately presented and dangerously close to being funny.

Then we work our socks off to get them out to you — at the cheapest possible prices.

Contents

☑ Use the tick boxes to help keep a record of which tests have been attempted.

Week 1
- ☐ Day 1 1
- ☐ Day 2 2
- ☐ Day 3 3
- ☐ Day 4 4
- ☐ Day 5 5

Week 2
- ☐ Day 1 6
- ☐ Day 2 7
- ☐ Day 3 8
- ☐ Day 4 9
- ☐ Day 5 10

Week 3
- ☐ Day 1 11
- ☐ Day 2 12
- ☐ Day 3 13
- ☐ Day 4 14
- ☐ Day 5 15

Week 4
- ☐ Day 1 16
- ☐ Day 2 17
- ☐ Day 3 18
- ☐ Day 4 19
- ☐ Day 5 20

Week 5
- ☐ Day 1 21
- ☐ Day 2 22
- ☐ Day 3 23
- ☐ Day 4 24
- ☐ Day 5 25

Week 6
- ☐ Day 1 26
- ☐ Day 2 27
- ☐ Day 3 28
- ☐ Day 4 29
- ☐ Day 5 30

Week 7
- ☐ Day 1 31
- ☐ Day 2 32
- ☐ Day 3 33
- ☐ Day 4 34
- ☐ Day 5 35

Week 8
- ☐ Day 1 36
- ☐ Day 2 37
- ☐ Day 3 38
- ☐ Day 4 39
- ☐ Day 5 40

Week 9

- [x] Day 1 41
- [x] Day 2 42
- [x] Day 3 43
- [x] Day 4 44
- [x] Day 5 45

Week 10

- [x] Day 1 46
- [x] Day 2 47
- [x] Day 3 48
- [x] Day 4 49
- [x] Day 5 50

Week 11

- [x] Day 1 51
- [x] Day 2 52
- [x] Day 3 53
- [x] Day 4 54
- [x] Day 5 55

Week 12

- [x] Day 1 56
- [x] Day 2 57
- [x] Day 3 58
- [x] Day 4 59
- [x] Day 5 60

Answers 61

Published by CGP

ISBN: 978 1 78908 657 7

Editors: Paul Jordin, Duncan Lindsay, Claire Plowman, Hannah Roscoe, James Summersgill

With thanks to Katie Fernandez and Alison Griffin for the proofreading.

With thanks to Lottie Edwards for the copyright research.

Clipart from Corel®

Printed by Elanders Ltd, Newcastle upon Tyne.
Based on the classic CGP style created by Richard Parsons.

Text, design, layout and original illustrations© Coordination Group Publications Ltd. (CGP) 2020
All rights reserved.

Photocopying this book is not permitted, even if you have a CLA licence.
Extra copies are available from CGP with next day delivery • 0800 1712 712 • www.cgpbooks.co.uk

How to Use this Book

- This book contains 60 daily practice tests.

- We've split them into 12 sections — that's roughly one for each week of the Year 5 summer term.

- Each week is made up of 5 tests, so there's one for every school day of the term (Monday – Friday).

- Each test should take about 10 minutes to complete.

- The tests contain a mix of topics from Year 5 Maths. New Year 5 topics are gradually introduced as you go through the book.

- The tests increase in difficulty as you progress through the term.

- The last three weeks recap topics from throughout Year 5 Maths.

- Each test looks something like this:

The Week and the Day of the test are shown at the top of the page.

There's an example at the top of the page. The correct answer is shown in red. Talk the pupil through the instruction and the example so they know what to do.

The instruction the pupil needs to follow is in the box at the top of the page.

Week 3 — Day 3

Look at the airport arrivals information. Write down what time the flight landed using the 24-hour clock.

The flight from Paris was due at 2:28 pm, but landed 15 minutes late.

14:43

① The flight from Berlin was due at 11:23 am, but landed 26 minutes late.

② The flight from Havana was due at 8:50 pm, but landed 35 minutes early.

③ The flight from Barcelona was due at 1:49 pm, but landed 12 minutes late.

④ The flight from Reykjavik was due at 6:05 pm, but landed 17 minutes early.

⑤ The flight from Boston was due at 5:58 am, but landed 38 minutes late.

⑥ The flight from Tokyo was due at 10:33 pm, but landed 45 minutes late.

⑦ The flight from Copenhagen was due at 12:07 am, but landed 18 minutes early.

⑧ The flight from Cairo was due at 11:47 pm, but landed 23 minutes late.

Today I scored ☐ out of 8.

There's a score box at the bottom of the test. Use this to keep track of how well the pupil has done.

There are between 4 and 12 questions for the pupil to answer.

Week 1 — Day 1

Use a protractor to measure the angle. 45°

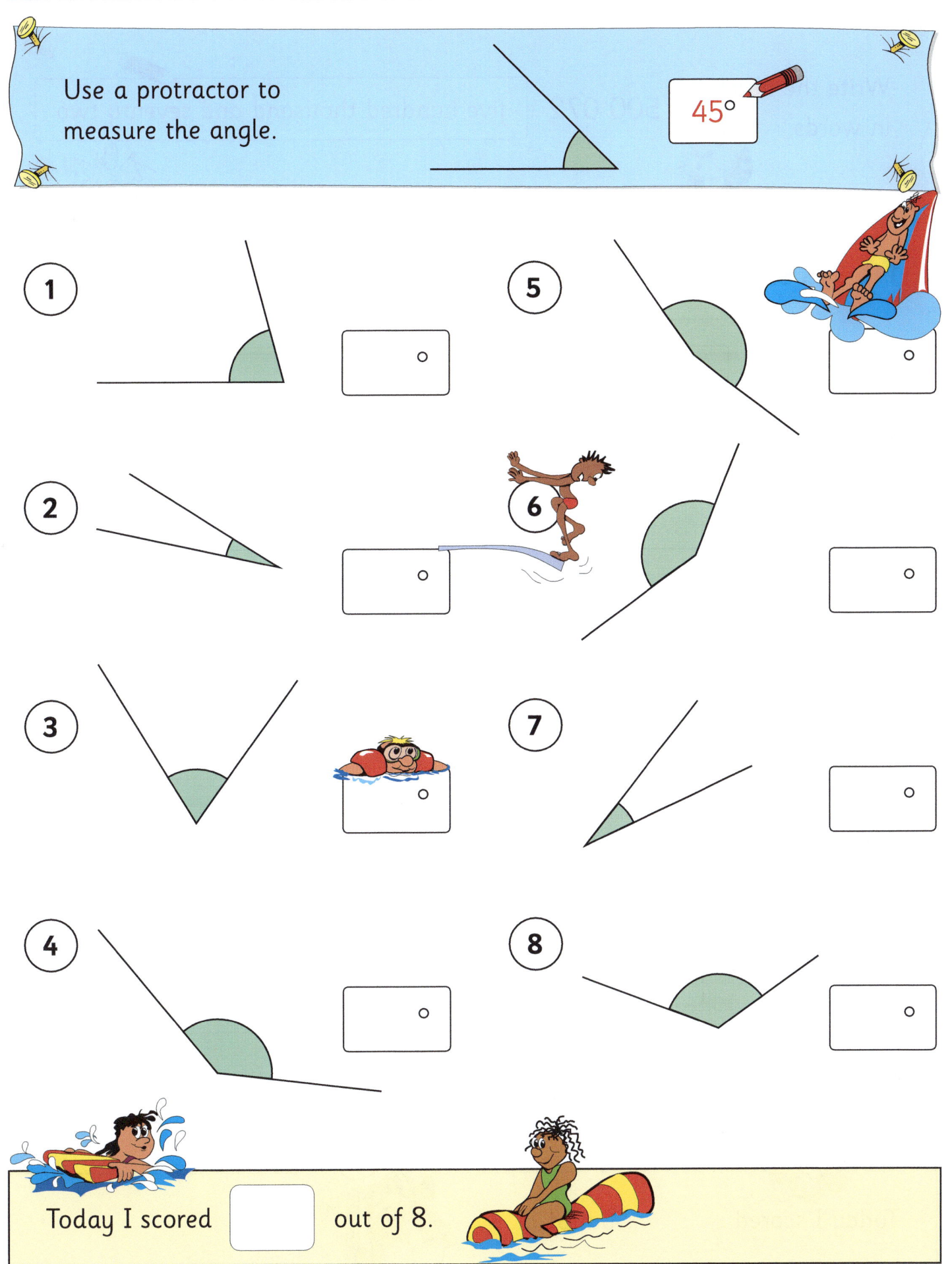

1.
2.
3.
4.
5.
6.
7.
8.

Today I scored ☐ out of 8.

Week 1 — Day 2

Write the number in words. 500 072 *five hundred thousand and seventy two*

1) 348 529

2) 264 087

3) 956 823

4) 880 244

5) 306 502

6) 1 473 001

7) 6 902 600

8) 3 067 809

Today I scored ☐ out of 8.

Week 1 — Day 3

Fill in the missing number.

There are 1200 aliens on a planet. 7 out of every 100 aliens are Zigs. How many Zigs are there on the planet?

84

1. There are 90 aliens on a planet. 3 out of every 10 aliens are Plinks. How many Plinks are there on the planet?

2. There are 450 aliens on a planet. 4 out of every 50 aliens are Yoys. How many Yoys are there on the planet?

3. There are 300 aliens on a planet. 9 out of every 20 aliens are Flumps. How many Flumps are there on the planet?

4. There are 2300 aliens on a planet. 6 out of every 100 aliens are Golgs. How many Golgs are there on the planet?

5. There are 600 aliens on a planet. 7 out of every 75 aliens are Jorgs. How many Jorgs are there on the planet?

6. There are 1750 aliens on a planet. 11 out of every 250 aliens are Sups. How many Sups are there on the planet?

7. There are 825 aliens on a planet. 8 out of every 25 aliens are Mofs. How many Mofs are there on the planet?

8. There are 504 aliens on a planet. 8 out of every 12 aliens are Tonks. How many Tonks are there on the planet?

Today I scored ☐ out of 8.

Week 1 — Day 4

Rani is making jugs of orange drink for a girls' basketball team. Work out how much squash she needs.

For 1 jug...
250 ml squash
1 l water

For 6 jugs, Rani needs 1.5 l of squash.

1 For 2 jugs...
325 ml squash
1.5 l water

For 6 jugs, Rani needs ☐ ml of squash.

2 For 1 jug...
280 ml squash
1.75 l water

For 1½ jugs, Rani needs ☐ ml of squash.

3 For 1 jug...
320 ml squash
2 l water

For 3½ jugs, Rani needs ☐ l of squash.

4 For 10 jugs...
3.5 l squash
12 l water

For 1 jug Rani needs ☐ ml of squash.

5 For 1 jug...
480 ml squash
3.8 l water

For 6¼ jugs, Rani needs ☐ l of squash.

6 For 1 jug...
440 ml squash
3.25 l water

For 9¾ jugs, Rani needs ☐ l of squash.

7 For 3 jugs...
660 ml squash
8.2 l water

For 11 jugs Rani needs ☐ l of squash.

8 For 2 jugs...
640 ml squash
7.5 l water

For 8½ jugs, Rani needs ☐ l of squash.

Today I scored ☐ out of 8.

Week 1 — Day 5

Class 5 are raising money by doing a sponsored walk. Fill in the missing number.

Amy gets £1.20 for every 1 km she walks. How far does Amy need to walk to raise £24?

20 km

1. Bilal gets £3 for every 5 km he walks. How far does Bilal need to walk to raise £15?

    ___ km

2. Caley gets 40p for every 1 km she walks. How far does Caley need to walk to raise £10?

    ___ km

3. Dexter gets 60p for every 2 km he walks. How far does Dexter need to walk to raise £18?

    ___ km

4. Freya gets £2.50 for every 4 km she walks. How far does Freya need to walk to raise £17.50?

    ___ km

5. Gaz gets £1.50 for every 3 km he walks. How far does Gaz need to walk to raise £16.50?

    ___ km

6. Haf gets £3.50 for every 6 km she walks. How far does Haf need to walk to raise £21?

    ___ km

7. Ian gets £2.20 for every 4 km he walks. How far does Ian need to walk to raise £19.80?

    ___ km

8. Jae gets 20p for every 500 m she walks. How far does Jae need to walk to raise £11.60?

    ___ km

Today I scored ___ out of 8.

Week 2 — Day 1

Rearrange the number cards to make a number that matches the description. Use each number card once.

8 3 4 6 → Make the smallest possible number. **3468**

1) 2 4 1 2 — Make the largest possible number.

2) 7 8 5 6 — Make the largest possible number with 6 in the thousands place.

3) 9 2 1 5 — Make the smallest possible number with 1 in the tens place.

4) 2 6 8 9 6 — Make the largest possible number.

5) 9 4 9 8 4 — Make the smallest possible number.

6) 6 7 5 4 5 — Make the smallest possible number with 4 in the tens place.

7) 2 3 1 8 3 — Make the largest possible number with 2 in the hundreds place.

8) 6 8 9 9 9 — Make the smallest possible number with 9 in the thousands place.

Today I scored ☐ out of 8.

Year 5 Maths — Summer Term

Week 2 — Day 2

Work out the length of side A. The shapes are not drawn to scale.

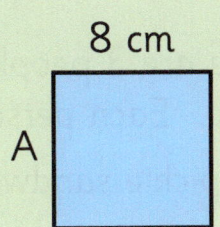
8 cm

The perimeter of the square is 32 cm. What is the length of side A?

A = 8 cm

1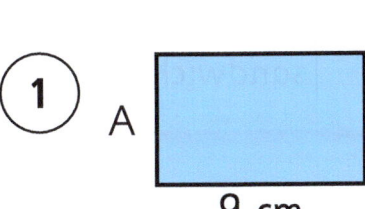

The perimeter of the rectangle is 28 cm. What is the length of side A?

A = ☐ cm

2

The perimeter of the square is 26.4 cm. What is the length of side A?

A = ☐ cm

3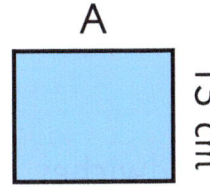

The perimeter of the rectangle is 0.7 m. What is the length of side A?

A = ☐ cm

4

The perimeter of the square is 0.176 m. What is the length of side A?

A = ☐ cm

5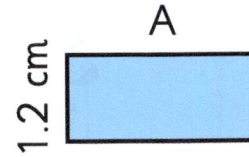

The perimeter of the rectangle is 0.222 m. What is the length of side A?

A = ☐ cm

Today I scored ☐ out of 5.

Week 2 — Day 3

How many sandwiches are eaten in total? Give your answer as a mixed number if possible.

There are 3 people at a picnic. Each person eats $2\frac{1}{2}$ pickle sandwiches.

$7\frac{1}{2}$ sandwiches

1. There are 4 people at a picnic. Each person eats $1\frac{1}{3}$ ham sandwiches.

    ☐ sandwiches

2. There are 5 people at a picnic. Each person eats $4\frac{1}{2}$ salmon sandwiches.

    ☐ sandwiches

3. There are 6 people at a picnic. Each person eats $\frac{1}{2}$ of a cheese sandwich and $1\frac{1}{2}$ beef sandwiches.

    ☐ sandwiches

4. There are 6 people at a picnic. Each person eats $2\frac{1}{4}$ egg sandwiches.

    ☐ sandwiches

5. There are 9 people at a picnic. Each person eats $3\frac{2}{5}$ cucumber sandwiches.

    ☐ sandwiches

6. There are 5 people at a picnic. Each person eats $\frac{2}{3}$ of a chicken sandwich and $\frac{5}{6}$ of a prawn sandwich.

    ☐ sandwiches

Today I scored ☐ out of 6.

Week 2 — Day 4

Write the Roman numeral in numbers.

MMX = 2010

1) MM =

2) MMVII =

3) MCMI =

4) MDCC =

5) MMXLV =

6) MCCXL =

7) MCMLXXX =

8) MDCCCXXII =

9) CMLXXVIII =

10) MCCCXXXIV =

11) DCCCLII =

12) MDCCCLXIX =

Today I scored ☐ out of 12.

Week 2 — Day 5

Write down how much the animal eats.

A tortoise eats 275 g of lettuce every day. How many kilograms of lettuce does it eat in 4 days?

1.1 kg

1) A lion eats 12 kg of meat every day. How many kilograms of meat does it eat in 9 days? ☐ kg

2) A monkey eats 500 g of bananas every day. How many kilograms of bananas does it eat in 6 days? ☐ kg

3) A giraffe eats 32 kg of leaves every day. How many kilograms of leaves does it eat in 4 days? ☐ kg

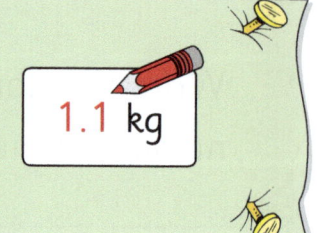

4) A rhino eats 66 kg of grass every day. How many kilograms of grass does it eat in 5 days? ☐ kg

5) A pig eats 800 g of apples every day. How many kilograms of apples does it eat in 7 days? ☐ kg

6) An elephant eats 174 kg of hay every day. How many kilograms of hay does it eat in 8 days? ☐ kg

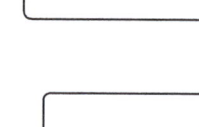

7) A penguin eats 945 g of fish every day. How many kilograms of fish does it eat in 7 days? ☐ kg

8) A panda eats 29.8 kg of bamboo every day. How many kilograms of bamboo does it eat in 12 days? ☐ kg

Today I scored ☐ out of 8.

Week 3 — Day 1

Use the conversion 1 m = 3 feet to convert the measurement.

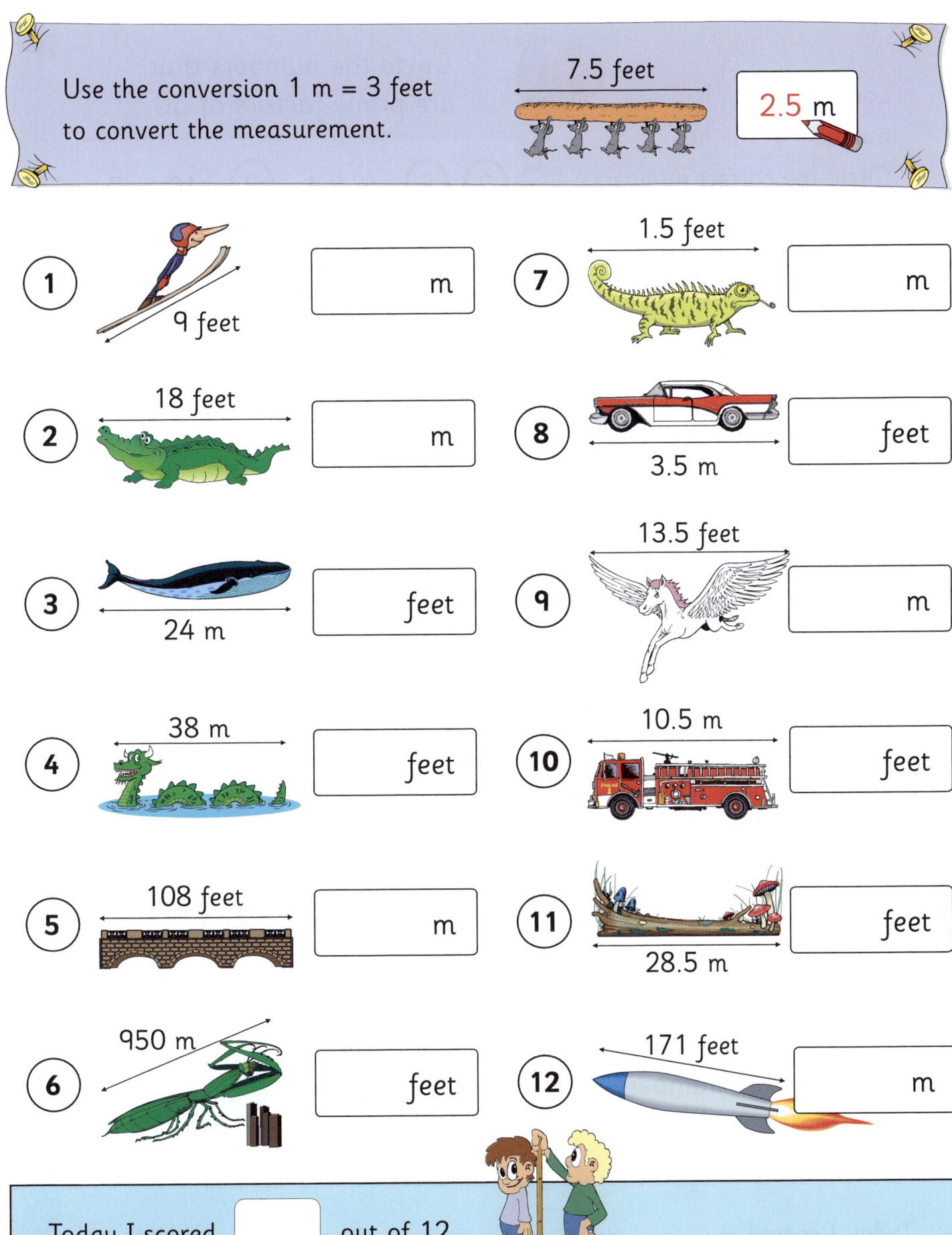

1. 9 feet → ___ m
2. 18 feet → ___ m
3. 24 m → ___ feet
4. 38 m → ___ feet
5. 108 feet → ___ m
6. 950 m → ___ feet
7. 1.5 feet → ___ m
8. 3.5 m → ___ feet
9. 13.5 feet → ___ m
10. 10.5 m → ___ feet
11. 28.5 m → ___ feet
12. 171 feet → ___ m

Today I scored ___ out of 12.

Week 3 — Day 2

Look at the numbers in the box. Circle the correct numbers.

Circle the numbers that are prime factors of 30.

② ⑤ 8 6 ③ 10 7

1) Circle the numbers that are prime factors of 20.

2 3 10 4 5 11

2) Circle the numbers that are prime factors of 77.

2 11 8 6 3 7

3) Circle the numbers that are prime factors of 100.

2 4 5 10 7 25 3

4) Circle the numbers that are prime factors of 99.

6 5 8 3 11 12 2

5) Circle the numbers that are prime factors of 84.

2 5 13 12 7 3 8

6) Circle the numbers that are prime factors of 52.

2 19 4 6 3 13 7

7) Circle the numbers that are prime factors of 60.

5 8 11 6 7 3 2

Today I scored ☐ out of 7.

Week 3 — Day 3

Look at the airport arrivals information. Write down what time the flight landed using the 24-hour clock.

The flight from Paris was due at 2:28 pm, but landed 15 minutes late.

14:43

1. The flight from Berlin was due at 11:23 am, but landed 26 minutes late.

2. The flight from Havana was due at 8:50 pm, but landed 35 minutes early.

3. The flight from Barcelona was due at 1:49 pm, but landed 12 minutes late.

4. The flight from Reykjavik was due at 6:05 pm, but landed 17 minutes early.

5. The flight from Boston was due at 5:58 am, but landed 38 minutes late.

6. The flight from Tokyo was due at 10:33 pm, but landed 45 minutes late.

7. The flight from Copenhagen was due at 12:07 am, but landed 18 minutes early.

8. The flight from Cairo was due at 11:47 pm, but landed 23 minutes late.

Today I scored ☐ out of 8.

Week 3 — Day 4

Find the answer that comes out of the number machine.

number of vertices of a pentagon → + number of edges of a square → × number of vertices of a hexagon → 54

1. number of vertices of a heptagon → − number of vertices of a triangle → × number of edges of a octagon → ☐

2. number of vertices of a kite → − number of vertices of an octagon → + number of edges of a hexagon → ☐

3. number of edges of a rectangle → + number of edges of an octagon → ÷ number of vertices of a square → ☐

4. number of edges of a heptagon → − number of vertices of a pentagon → × number of edges of a hexagon → ☐

5. number of vertices of an octagon → × number of edges in a hexagon → ÷ number of edges of a trapezium → ☐

6. number of vertices of a rhombus → + number of edges of a pentagon → × number of vertices of a heptagon → ☐

Today I scored ☐ out of 6.

Week 3 — Day 5

Write down the number that matches the description.

I've got two digits. I'm a prime factor of 66.

1 I'm an even number. I'm a prime number.

2 I'm between 13 and 20. My only prime factors are 2 and 3.

3 I'm an odd number. I'm a factor of 26.

4 I'm a non-prime factor of 45. I have one digit.

5 I'm the greatest prime factor of 42.

6 I'm the smallest prime number that isn't a factor of 30.

7 I'm a non-prime factor of 12 and 20.

8 I've got the same prime factors as 20, but I'm less than 20.

Today I scored ☐ out of 8.

Week 4 — Day 1

Fill in the missing numbers in the sequence.   39, 32, 25, **18**, **11**, **4**, **−3**

1) 34, 29, 24, ☐, ☐, ☐, ☐

2) 29, 23, 17, ☐, ☐, ☐, ☐

3) 81, 66, 51, ☐, ☐, ☐, ☐

4) 54, 43, 32, ☐, ☐, ☐, ☐

5) 127, 105, 83, ☐, ☐, ☐, ☐

6) 97, 78, 59, ☐, ☐, ☐, ☐

7) 316, 262, 208, ☐, ☐, ☐, ☐

8) 256, 213, 170, ☐, ☐, ☐, ☐

Today I scored ☐ out of 8.

Week 4 — Day 2

Work out the size of angle X. [diagram: 68°, X, 27°] → **85°**

Today I scored ☐ out of 12.

Week 4 — Day 3

The table shows the number of flowers sold by a florist. How many more flowers did they sell in weeks 3 and 4 than in weeks 1 and 2?

Week	1	2	3	4
Flowers Sold	7025	4998	8652	7406

4035

1)
Week	1	2	3	4
Flowers Sold	1465	2222	5439	4982

2)
Week	1	2	3	4
Flowers Sold	2087	3504	5511	6007

3)
Week	1	2	3	4
Flowers Sold	5882	4038	6161	7443

4)
Week	1	2	3	4
Flowers Sold	5001	3289	9057	1654

5)
Week	1	2	3	4
Flowers Sold	460	8012	4368	5685

6)
Week	1	2	3	4
Flowers Sold	9021	6608	8227	8964

7)
Week	1	2	3	4
Flowers Sold	6518	8672	7264	8445

8)
Week	1	2	3	4
Flowers Sold	9826	8973	9999	8859

Today I scored ☐ out of 8.

Week 4 — Day 4

Circle the square number in the list.   19   (25)   6   24

1. 10   8   4   2
2. 11   20   14   9
3. 33   36   28   31
4. 16   21   15   12
5. 7   1   5   3
6. 49   44   42   52
7. 50   64   68   66
8. 91   77   89   100
9. 81   85   56   99
10. 101   121   114   123

Today I scored ☐ out of 10.

Week 4 — Day 5

Circle the option which is equivalent to the calculation in the pink box.

3^3

3 + 3 + 3 | **(3 × 3 × 3)** | 3 × 3

1) 2^3 — 2 + 3 | 2 × 2 | 2 × 2 × 2

2) 8^2 — 8 + 8 | 8 × 2 | 8 × 8 | 8 ÷ 2

3) 1^3 — 3 + 1 | 1 | 1 × 3 | 13

4) 7^2 — 72 | 2 × 7 | 49 | 7 + 7

5) $3^2 + 2^2$ — 5 × 2 | 6 + 4 | 25 | 9 + 4

6) 5^3 — 3 ÷ 5 | 5 × 25 | 3 × 5 | 53

7) 9^2 — 4.5 | 99 | 18 | 81

8) $4^3 - 1^3$ — 64 − 1 | 3^3 | 9 | 4 ÷ 3

Today I scored ☐ out of 8.

Week 5 — Day 1

Some people have been on holiday. Fill in the day of the week that they return.

Monday 29th June → **Sunday** 5th July

1) Monday 25th November → ☐ 30th November

2) Tuesday 13th August → ☐ 19th August

3) Saturday 25th December → ☐ 4th January

4) Wednesday 24th April → ☐ 7th May

5) Sunday 27th January → ☐ 6th February

6) Thursday 26th July → ☐ 10th August

7) Friday 28th September → ☐ 3rd October

8) Monday 25th May → ☐ 13th June

Today I scored ☐ out of 8.

Week 5 — Day 2

Fill in the missing number. $72 \div \boxed{8} = 3^2$

1) $7^2 \times 3 = \boxed{}$

2) $2^3 \times 4 = \boxed{}$

3) $8^3 \div 2^3 = \boxed{}$

4) $10^3 \div 5^3 = \boxed{}$

5) $4^2 \times \boxed{} = 80$

6) $200 \div \boxed{} = 5^2$

7) $\boxed{} \div 2 = 8^2$

8) $54 \div 2 = \boxed{}^3$

9) $\boxed{}^3 \times 3^2 = 72$

10) $196 \div 4 = \boxed{}^2$

11) $2^2 \times \boxed{}^2 = 6^2$

12) $6^3 \times \boxed{} = 432$

Today I scored $\boxed{}$ out of 12.

Week 5 — Day 3

12 inches is approximately equal to 30 centimetres. Circle the correct conversion.

6 inches in centimetres is

(15 cm)   25 cm   20 cm

1) 10 centimetres in inches is

3 in   4 in   2 in

2) 24 inches in centimetres is

90 cm   45 cm   60 cm

3) 120 centimetres in inches is

48 in   10 in   60 in

4) 120 inches in centimetres is

100 cm   50 cm   300 cm

5) 150 centimetres in inches is

50 in   60 in   30 in

6) 36 inches in centimetres is

95 cm   90 cm   80 cm

7) 40 centimetres in inches is

10 in   16 in   14 in

8) 18 inches in centimetres is

34 cm   38 cm   45 cm

9) 75 centimetres in inches is

36 in   28 in   30 in

10) 54 inches in centimetres is

135 cm   96 cm   99 cm

11) 200 centimetres in inches is

72 in   80 in   81 in

12) 20 inches in centimetres is

48 cm   53 cm   50 cm

Today I scored ☐ out of 12.

Week 5 — Day 4

Put the fractions in order starting with the **smallest**.

$\frac{7}{10}$ $\frac{3}{10}$ $\frac{4}{20}$ $\frac{2}{5}$

$\frac{4}{20}$ $\frac{3}{10}$ $\frac{2}{5}$ $\frac{7}{10}$

1) $\frac{5}{8}$ $\frac{3}{4}$ $\frac{7}{8}$ $\frac{1}{4}$

5) $\frac{1}{2}$ $\frac{3}{8}$ $\frac{1}{4}$ $\frac{10}{16}$

2) $\frac{1}{6}$ $\frac{5}{6}$ $\frac{1}{3}$ $\frac{2}{3}$

6) $\frac{13}{20}$ $\frac{7}{10}$ $\frac{6}{40}$ $\frac{4}{5}$

3) $\frac{5}{6}$ $\frac{1}{12}$ $\frac{17}{24}$ $\frac{5}{12}$

7) $\frac{7}{10}$ $\frac{17}{50}$ $\frac{33}{100}$ $\frac{47}{50}$

4) $\frac{16}{36}$ $\frac{5}{18}$ $\frac{7}{18}$ $\frac{7}{9}$

8) $\frac{16}{56}$ $\frac{3}{28}$ $\frac{5}{7}$ $\frac{5}{14}$

Today I scored ☐ out of 8.

Week 5 — Day 5

How many people bought a burger? There were 40 000 people at a festival. $\frac{3}{4}$ bought lunch. $\frac{1}{3}$ of the people who bought lunch bought a burger.

10 000

1. There were 60 000 people at a concert. $\frac{1}{2}$ bought food. $\frac{1}{10}$ of the people who bought food bought a burger.

2. There were 80 000 people at a fair. $\frac{1}{4}$ bought lunch. $\frac{1}{5}$ of the people who bought lunch bought a burger.

3. There were 90 000 people at a rally. $\frac{1}{3}$ bought a snack. $\frac{1}{10}$ of the people who bought a snack bought a burger.

4. There were 120 000 people at a festival. $\frac{2}{3}$ bought dinner. $\frac{1}{4}$ of the people who bought dinner bought a burger.

5. There were 100 000 people at a game. $\frac{3}{4}$ bought a snack. $\frac{1}{5}$ of the people who bought a snack bought a burger.

6. There were 200 000 people in a park. $\frac{7}{10}$ bought food. $\frac{3}{4}$ of the people who bought food bought a burger.

Today I scored ⬜ out of 6.

Week 6 — Day 1

Calculate the area of the rectangle.
The rectangle is not drawn to scale.

9 cm × 4 cm → 36 cm²

1. 7 cm × 6 cm = ___ cm²
2. 3 cm × 8 cm = ___ cm²
3. 9 cm × 11 cm = ___ cm²
4. 12 cm × 5 cm = ___ cm²
5. 8 cm × 5 cm = ___ cm²
6. 3 cm × 13 cm = ___ cm²
7. 12 cm × 7 cm = ___ cm²
8. 4 cm × 15 cm = ___ cm²
9. 14 cm × 6 cm = ___ cm²
10. 17 cm × 3 cm = ___ cm²
11. 8 cm × 13 cm = ___ cm²
12. 5 cm × 16 cm = ___ cm²

Today I scored ___ out of 12.

Week 6 — Day 2

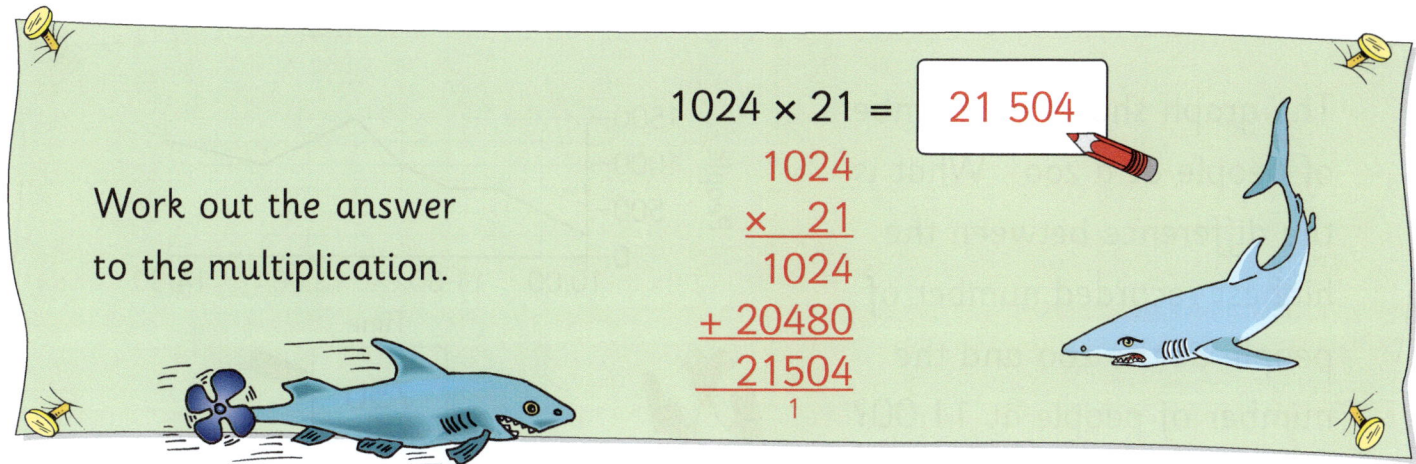

Work out the answer to the multiplication.

1024 × 21 = 21 504

```
   1024
 ×   21
   1024
 +20480
  21504
      1
```

1) 356 × 17 =

2) 482 × 39 =

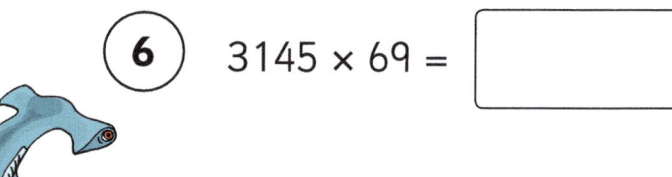

3) 2791 × 52 =

4) 1164 × 26 =

5) 2807 × 53 =

6) 3145 × 69 =

7) 7523 × 74 =

8) 8396 × 48 =

Today I scored ☐ out of 8.

Week 6 — Day 3

The graph shows the number of people at a zoo. What is the difference between the highest recorded number of people at the zoo and the number of people at 11:00?

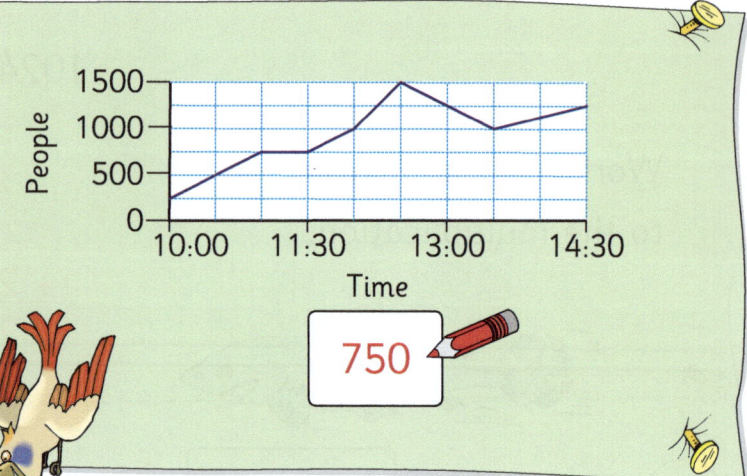

750

1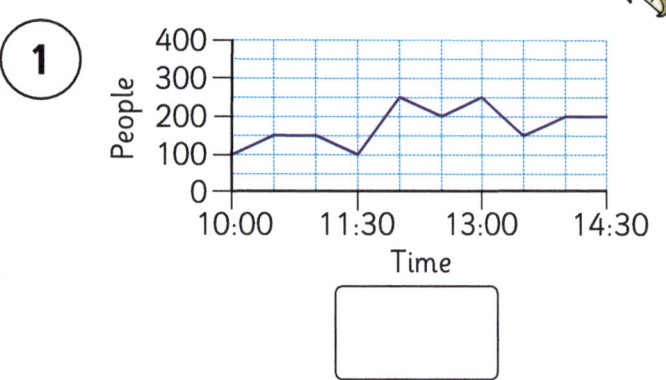

2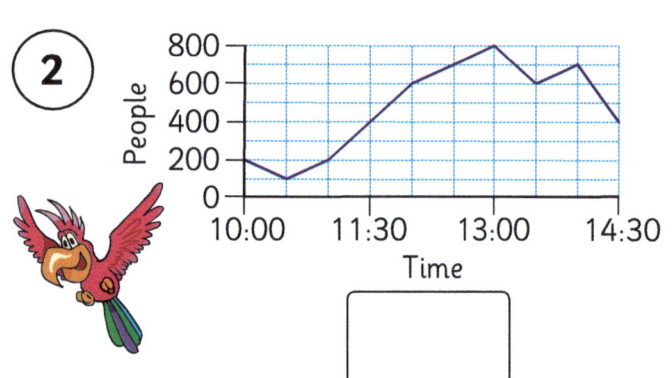

3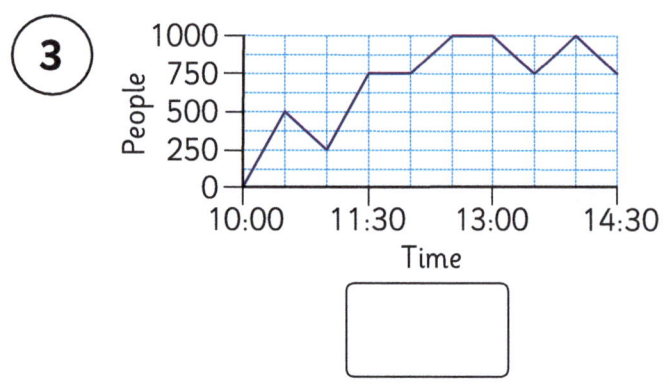

4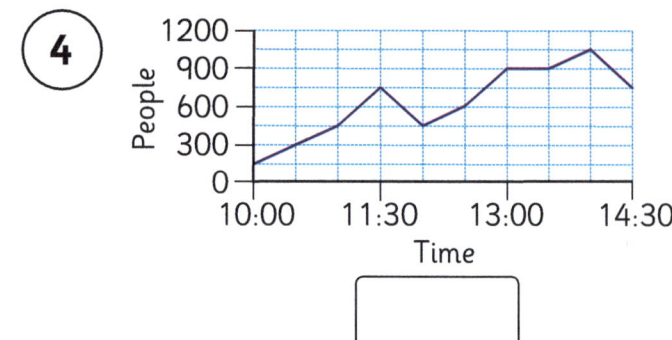

5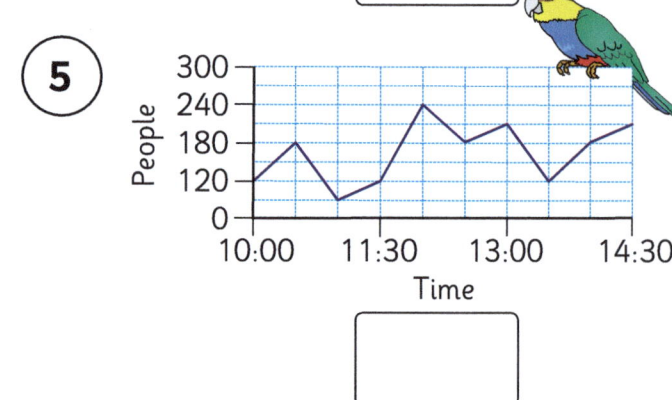

6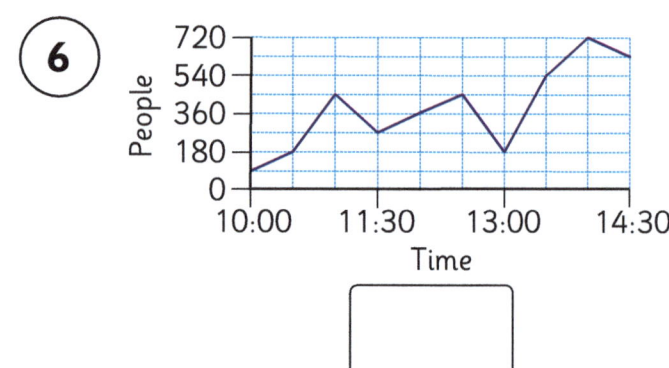

Today I scored ☐ out of 6.

Week 6 — Day 4

Write the measurements in the units given.

4.5 litres = 4500 ml

1) 170 cm = ☐ m

2) 2800 g = ☐ kg

3) 5000 m = ☐ km

4) 4.2 km = ☐ m

5) 3600 ml = ☐ litres

6) 1.25 m = ☐ cm

7) 9.1 kg = ☐ g

8) 10 litres = ☐ ml

9) 432 cm = ☐ m

10) 1150 g = ☐ kg

11) 2.61 km = ☐ m

12) 7300 ml = ☐ litres

Today I scored ☐ out of 12.

Week 6 — Day 5

How many bricks will be left in the box?

Ian has a box of toy bricks. 1021 are red and 3683 are blue. He uses half the bricks to build a spaceship.

2352

1. Brianna has a box of toy bricks. 1948 are orange and 2016 are purple. She uses half the bricks to build a rocket.

2. Abed has a box of toy bricks. 1753 are yellow and 1101 are white. He uses half the bricks to build an alien.

3. Lubna has a box of toy bricks. 3460 are red and 1828 are yellow. She uses half the bricks to build a planet.

4. Gemma has a box of toy bricks. 2913 are blue and 1769 are grey. She uses half the bricks to build a satellite.

5. Ichiro has a box of toy bricks. 1455 are green and 2083 are black. He uses half the bricks to build a spaceship.

6. Luke has a box of toy bricks. 2242 are purple and 2156 are blue. He uses half the bricks to build a rocket.

7. Hannah has a box of toy bricks. 1933 are orange and 3045 are red. She uses half the bricks to build an alien.

8. Yusra has a box of toy bricks. 2619 are grey and 2877 are green. She uses half the bricks to build a planet.

Today I scored ☐ out of 8.

Week 7 — Day 1

Circle the fractions that are equivalent to the number in the green box.

0.3 | (3/10) | 30/10 | 3/100 | (300/1000)

1. 0.1 | 100/10 | 1/10 | 100/1000 | 10/10 | 10/100

2. 0.4 | 400/1000 | 80/100 | 4/10 | 40/100 | 400/100

3. 0.6 | 9/10 | 600/1000 | 300/1000 | 60/100 | 60/10

4. 0.5 | 1/2 | 2/10 | 50/10 | 500/1000 | 50/100

5. 0.2 | 5/10 | 2/10 | 1/5 | 200/100 | 200/1000

6. 0.8 | 800/1000 | 4/10 | 40/50 | 80/10 | 8/100

7. 1.1 | 11/100 | 1/11 | 22/20 | 11/10 | 1100/1000

8. 0.9 | 1/9 | 90/100 | 900/100 | 1900/1000 | 900/1000

9. 1.5 | 15/10 | 30/200 | 1500/100 | 1500/1000 | 150/1000

10. 1.2 | 60/10 | 120/1000 | 240/200 | 6/5 | 1200/1000

Today I scored ☐ out of 10.

Week 7 — Day 2

The mirror line is shown by a dashed blue line. Reflect shape A in the mirror line.

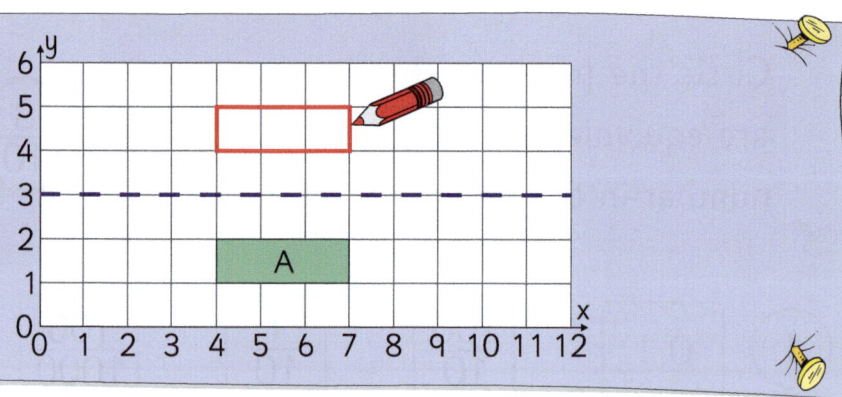

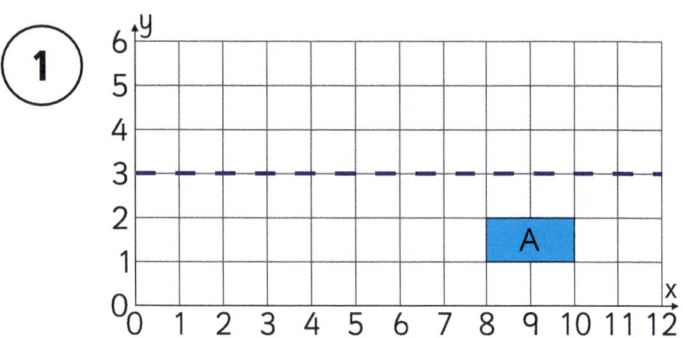

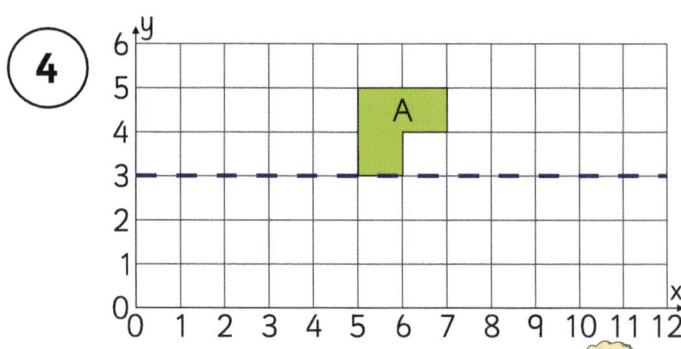

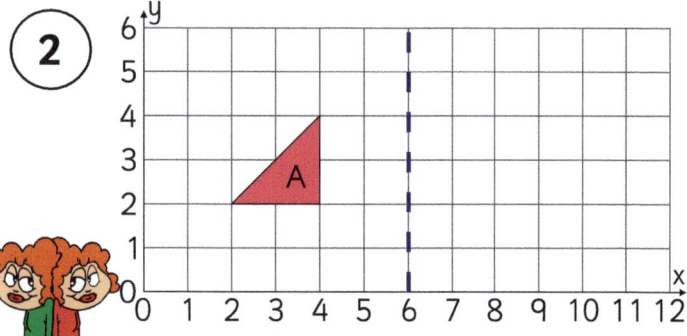

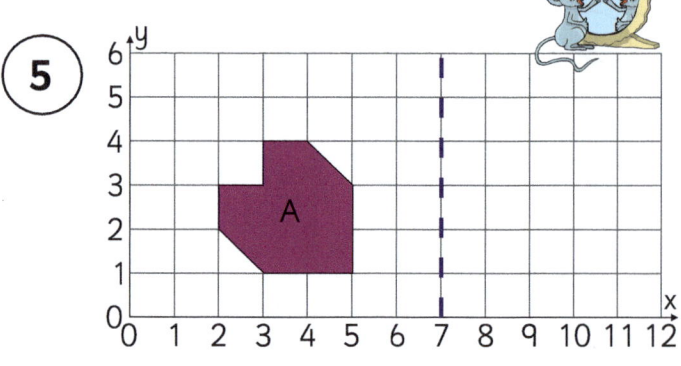

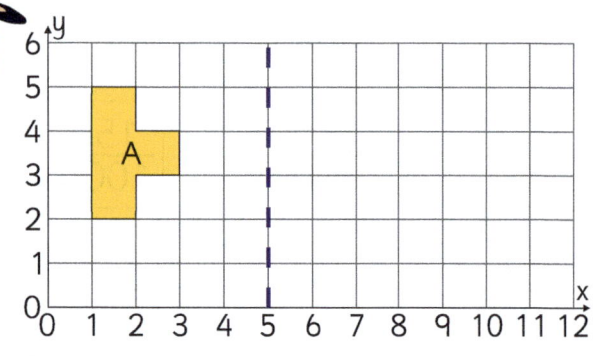

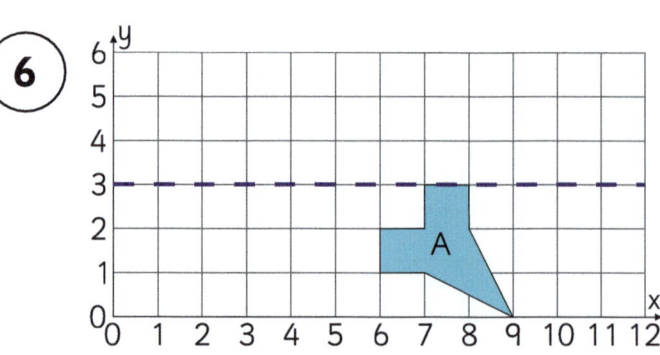

Today I scored ☐ out of 6.

Week 7 — Day 3

Write the fraction as a decimal.

$\frac{506}{1000}$ = 0.506

1. $\frac{123}{1000}$ =

2. $\frac{470}{1000}$ =

3. $\frac{698}{1000}$ =

4. $\frac{902}{1000}$ =

5. $\frac{1084}{1000}$ =

6. $\frac{1205}{1000}$ =

7. $\frac{1980}{1000}$ =

8. $\frac{92}{1000}$ =

9. $\frac{3419}{1000}$ =

10. $\frac{40}{1000}$ =

11. $\frac{6001}{1000}$ =

12. $\frac{7068}{1000}$ =

Today I scored ☐ out of 12.

Week 7 — Day 4

Write down the number of squares moved by shape A in each translation.

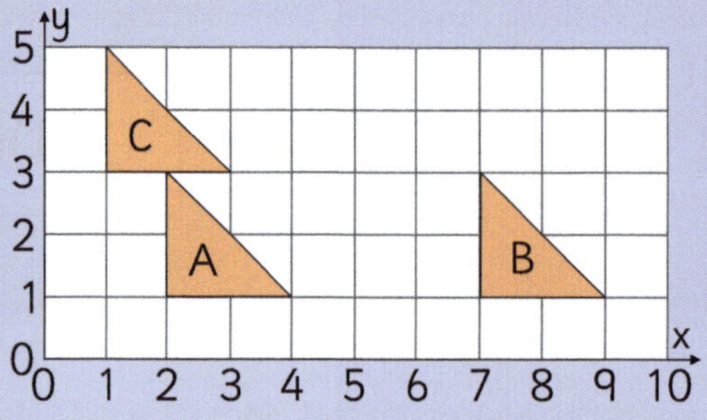

Shape A to B: **5 right**

Shape A to C: **1 left and 2 up**

1) Shape A to B:

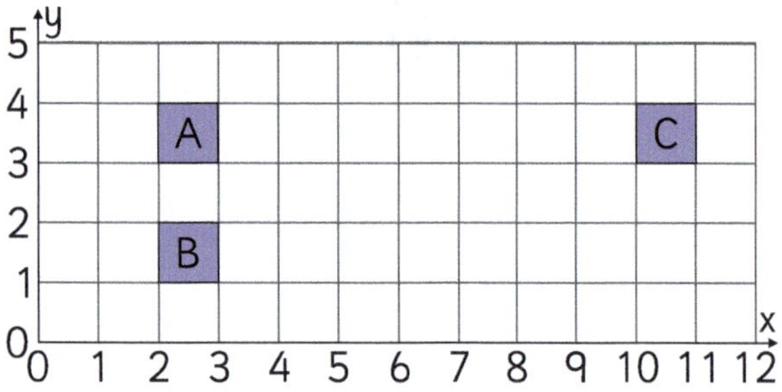

Shape A to C:

2) 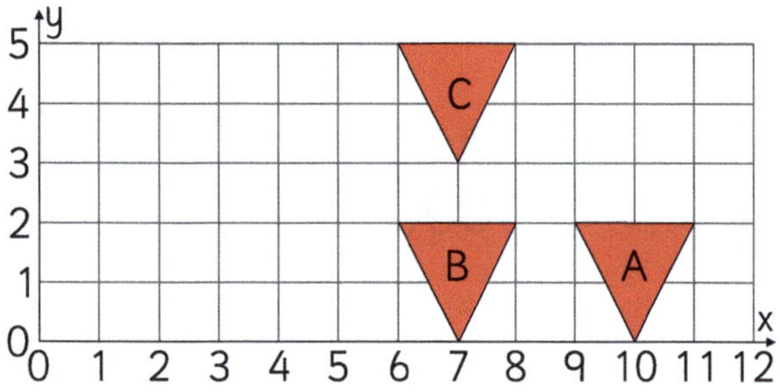 Shape A to B:

Shape A to C:

3)  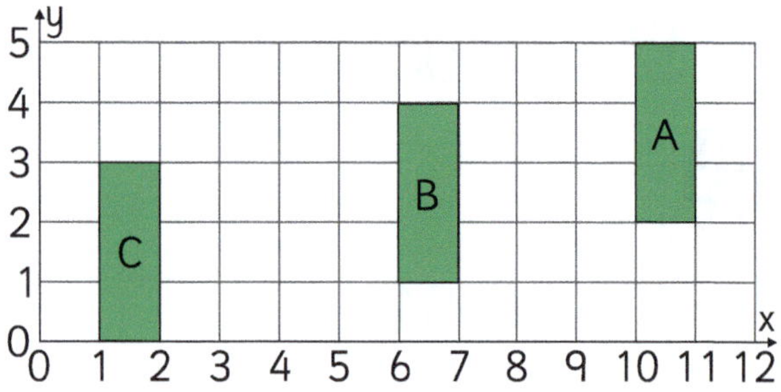 Shape A to B:

Shape A to C:

4) Shape A to B:

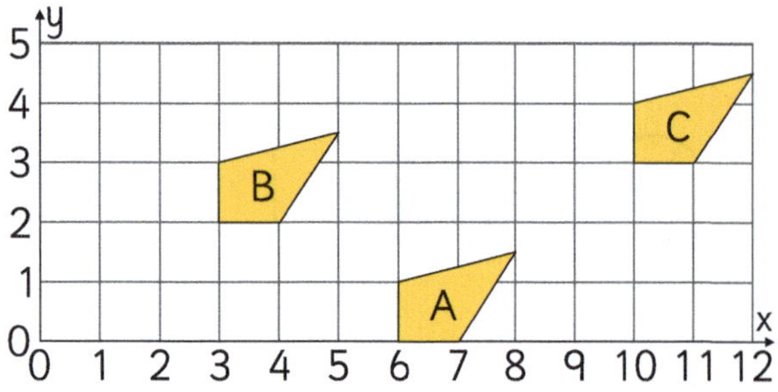

Shape A to C:

Today I scored ☐ out of 4.

Week 7 — Day 5

A cafe starts each day with three whole cakes. Which cake was there most left of at the end of the day?

On Sunday, the cafe sold $\frac{2}{12}$ of a coffee cake, $\frac{1}{3}$ of a ginger cake and $\frac{3}{6}$ of a carrot cake.

coffee

1) On Monday, the cafe sold $\frac{1}{2}$ of a vanilla cake, $\frac{3}{4}$ of a toffee cake and $\frac{2}{8}$ of a coffee cake.

2) On Tuesday, the cafe sold $\frac{2}{5}$ of an orange cake, $\frac{1}{3}$ of a lemon cake and $\frac{8}{15}$ of a strawberry cake.

3) On Wednesday, the cafe sold $\frac{11}{16}$ of a fudge cake, $\frac{1}{4}$ of a raspberry cake and $\frac{5}{8}$ of a banana cake.

4) On Thursday, the cafe sold $\frac{13}{20}$ of an apple cake, $\frac{3}{5}$ of a walnut cake and $\frac{9}{10}$ of a carrot cake.

5) On Friday, the cafe sold $\frac{5}{6}$ of a chocolate cake, $\frac{8}{12}$ of a lemon cake and $\frac{17}{24}$ of a toffee cake.

6) On Saturday, the cafe sold $\frac{11}{14}$ of an orange cake, $\frac{20}{28}$ of a vanilla cake and $\frac{4}{7}$ of a strawberry cake.

Today I scored ☐ out of 6.

Week 8 — Day 1

Circle the largest number.   1.380   1.083   (1.803)

1) 2.047   2.077   2.017
2) 5.911   5.191   5.991
3) 4.382   4.328   4.362
4) 3.061   3.081   3.031
5) 7.758   7.755   7.757
6) 1.249   1.429   1.424
7) 9.306   9.036   9.302
8) 6.244   6.241   6.242
9) 1.397   1.937   1.973
10) 2.865   2.586   2.856
11) 4.514   4.541   4.154
12) 8.188   8.881   8.818

Today I scored ☐ out of 12.

Week 8 — Day 2

How many metres of ribbon does the person have in total?

Carla has 2.164 m of ribbon. She buys another 1.5 m of ribbon.

3.664 m

1. Sanjay has 3.051 m of ribbon. He buys another 2.8 m of ribbon.

   ___ m

2. Peter has 2.772 m of ribbon. He buys another 1.2 m of ribbon.

   ___ m

3. Nisha has 1.408 m of ribbon. She buys another 3.3 m of ribbon.

   ___ m

4. Lauren has 4.293 m of ribbon. She buys another 1.6 m of ribbon.

   ___ m

5. Neil has 1.398 m of ribbon. He buys another 3.7 m of ribbon.

   ___ m

6. Mobeen has 3.182 m of ribbon. She buys another 3.31 m of ribbon.

   ___ m

7. Stuart has 2.537 m of ribbon. He buys another 4.08 m of ribbon.

   ___ m

8. Kylie has 5.469 m of ribbon. She buys another 2.54 m of ribbon.

   ___ m

Today I scored ___ out of 8.

Week 8 — Day 3

The table shows how long it took a teacher to mark some tests. How much longer did it take to mark the English tests than the Maths tests in minutes?

History	2 hrs 25 mins
English	2 hrs 3 mins
Maths	1 hr 26 mins

37 minutes

1.
Science	1 hr 36 mins
Maths	1 hr 7 mins
English	2 hrs 23 mins

_____ minutes

2.
English	2 hrs 47 mins
Geography	1 hr 15 mins
Maths	1 hr 41 mins

_____ minutes

3.
French	1 hr 23 mins
Maths	1 hr 59 mins
English	2 hrs 34 mins

_____ minutes

4.
English	2 hrs 58 mins
Maths	1 hr 39 mins
Spanish	2 hrs 12 mins

_____ minutes

5.
German	2 hrs 33 mins
English	3 hrs 2 mins
Maths	1 hr 28 mins

_____ minutes

6.
English	3 hrs 48 mins
Science	2 hrs 3 mins
Maths	1 hr 54 mins

_____ minutes

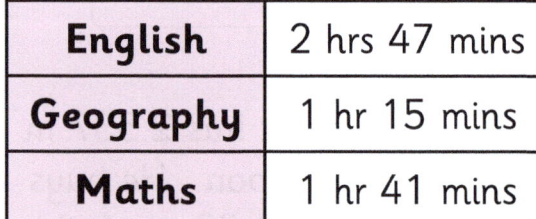

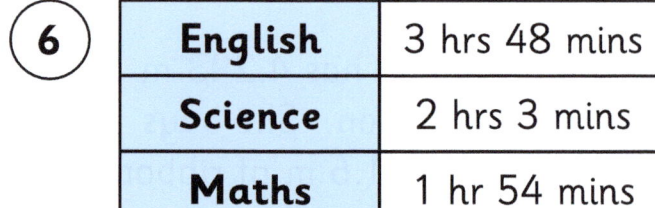

Today I scored ____ out of 6.

Week 8 — Day 4

Work out the answer to the question.

There are 56 biscuits in a tin. Marlon and his family eat $\frac{2}{7}$ of them. How many biscuits do they eat?

16

1) Robin has 420 ml of milk. She uses $\frac{4}{6}$ of it in a milkshake. How much milk does she use?

☐ ml

2) There are 93 cows on a farm. The farmer milks $\frac{1}{3}$ of them. How many cows does she milk?

☐

3) Mo has 2.8 m of tin foil. He uses $\frac{3}{4}$ of it to make a robot costume. How much foil does he use?

☐ m

4) Zayna has bought 54 carrots. She uses $\frac{3}{9}$ of them in a soup. How many carrots does she use?

☐

5) A kennel looks after 105 dogs. $\frac{2}{5}$ of them are poodles. How many poodles are there?

☐

6) There are 91 flowers in a field. $\frac{1}{7}$ of them are sunflowers. How many sunflowers are there?

☐

7) Louise has 336 g of flour. She needs $\frac{2}{3}$ of it for a cake. How much flour does she need?

☐ g

8) A shop has 112 gel pens. $\frac{6}{8}$ of them are green. How many gel pens are green?

☐

Today I scored ☐ out of 8.

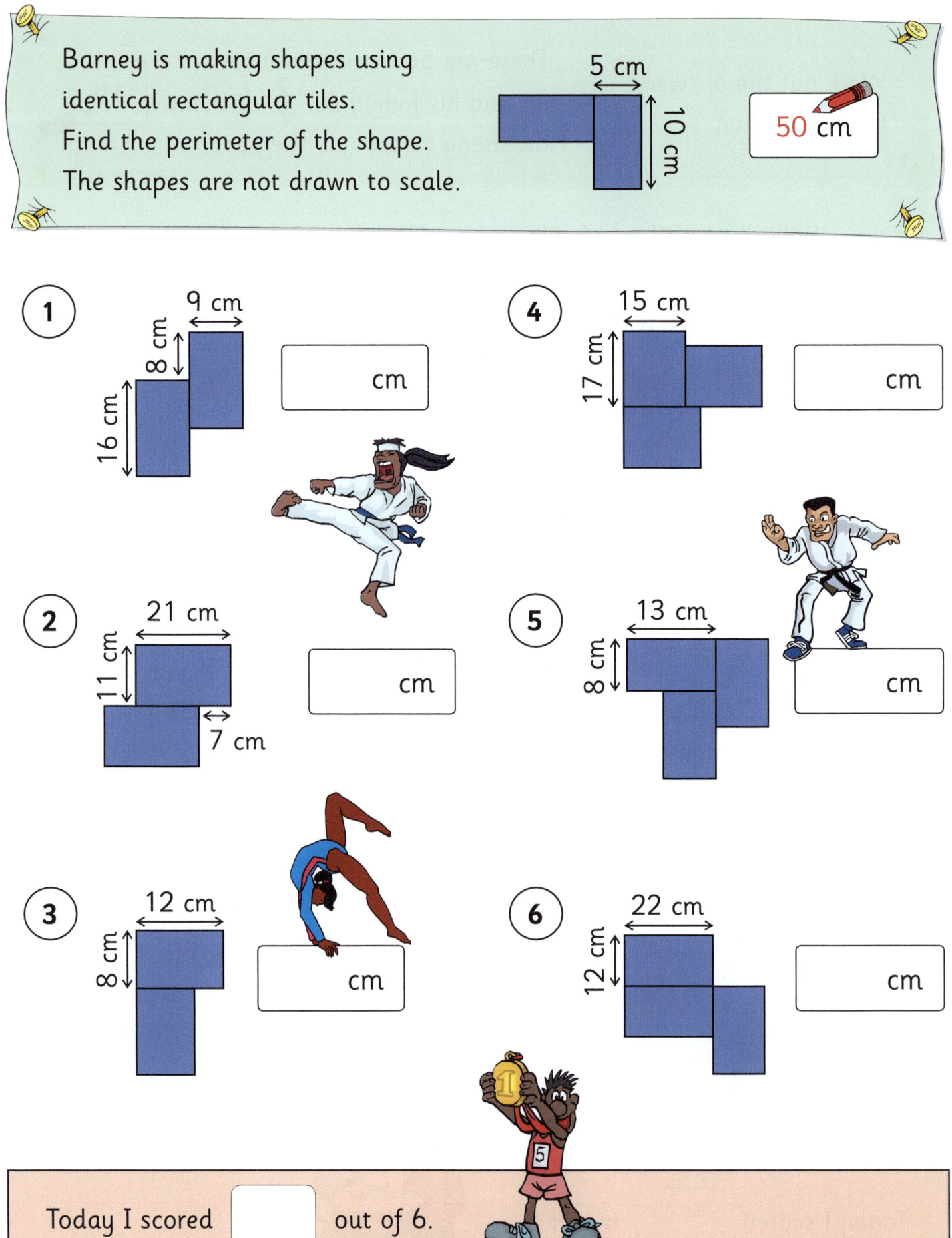

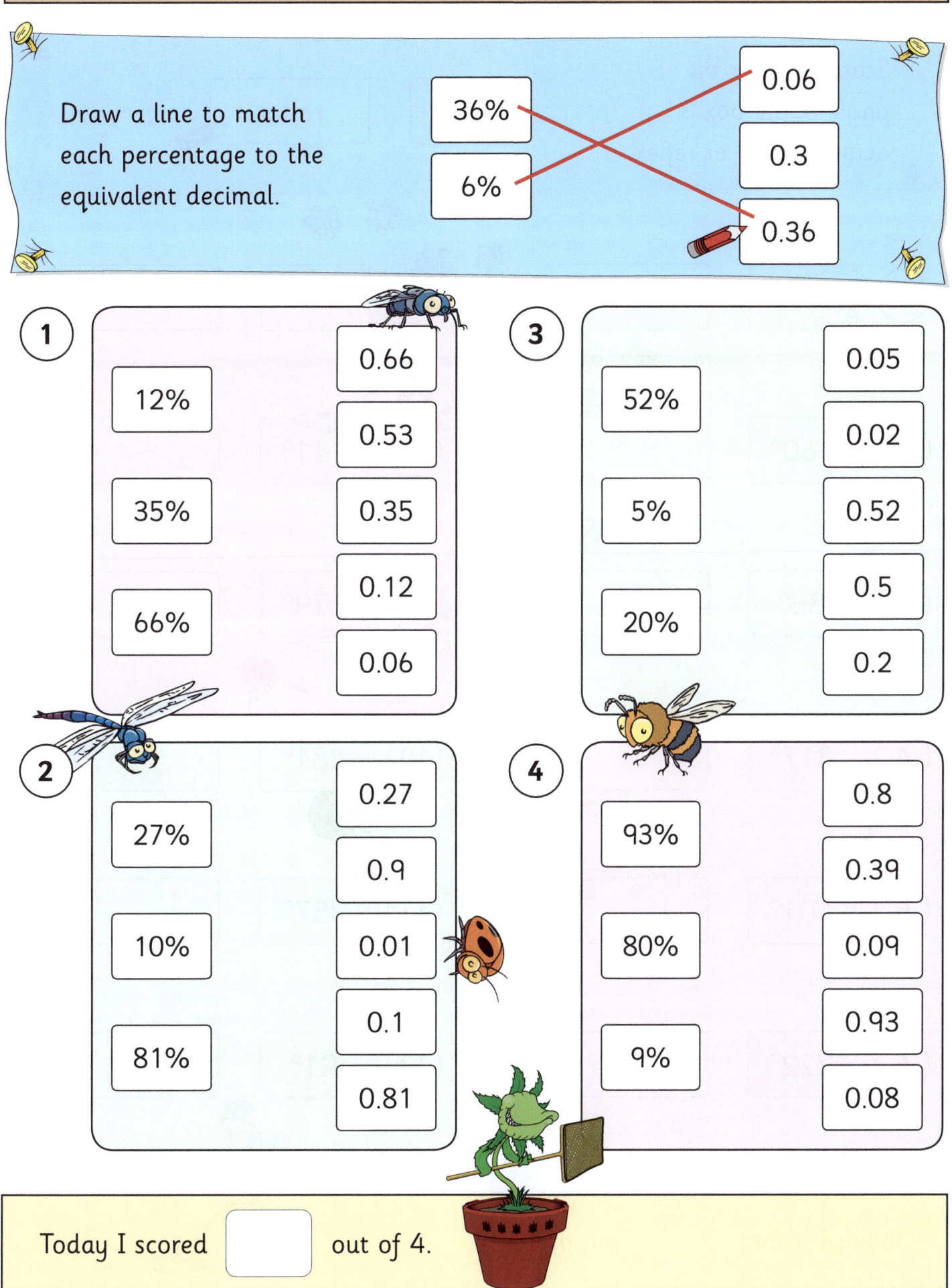

Week 9 — Day 2

State whether the angle in the box is acute, obtuse or reflex.

183° → reflex

1. 16° →
2. 160° →
3. 85° →
4. 317° →
5. 101° →
6. 222° →
7. 73° →
8. 141° →
9. 179° →
10. 281° →
11. 357° →
12. 91° →

Today I scored ☐ out of 12.

Week 9 — Day 3

Write the answer to the question.

Kevin had £100. He spent £43. What percentage of his money did he spend?

43%

1. Ana had £100. She spent £25. What percentage of her money did she spend?
___ %

2. Bev had £100. She spent 33% of her money. How much money did she spend?
£ ___

3. Chris had £10. He spent 20% of his money. How much money did he spend?
£ ___

4. Dia had £10. She spent £7. What percentage of her money did she spend?
___ %

5. Eli had £200. He spent £40. What percentage of his money did he spend?
___ %

6. Fliss had £200. She spent £8. What percentage of her money did she spend?
___ %

7. Gill had £200. She spent 60% of her money. How much money did she spend?
£ ___

8. Hasan had £200. He spent 11% of his money. How much money did he spend?
£ ___

9. Ira had £50. He spent £39. What percentage of his money did he spend?
___ %

10. Joan had £50. She spent 86% of her money. How much money did she spend?
£ ___

Today I scored ___ out of 10.

Week 9 — Day 4

Circle the smallest value in the list. | 42% | 0.48 | (4/10) |

1. | 0.25 | 15% | 20/100 |

2. | 55/100 | 0.45 | 50% |

3. | 10% | 0.19 | 16/100 |

4. | 0.29 | 3/10 | 33% |

5. | 6/10 | 58% | 0.64 |

6. | 89% | 9/10 | 0.93 |

7. | 54% | 0.57 | 1/2 |

8. | 0.79 | 4/5 | 72% |

9. | 1/4 | 0.21 | 24% |

10. | 75% | 0.73 | 35/50 |

11. | 12/20 | 0.57 | 68% |

12. | 3% | 0.05 | 1/25 |

Today I scored ☐ out of 12.

Week 9 — Day 5

Tina is making smoothies. Work out how many berries she needs in total.

For 1 smoothie:
10 raspberries
15 blueberries

For 12 smoothies she needs **300** berries.

1. For 1 smoothie: 11 strawberries, 12 blueberries. For 10 smoothies she needs ☐ berries.

2. For 2 smoothies: 19 strawberries, 26 raspberries. For 8 smoothies she needs ☐ berries.

3. For 5 smoothies: 52 blueberries, 41 raspberries. For 15 smoothies she needs ☐ berries.

4. For 1 smoothie: 17 blueberries, 14 raspberries. For 7 smoothies she needs ☐ berries.

5. For 3 smoothies: 37 strawberries, 29 gooseberries. For 9 smoothies she needs ☐ berries.

6. For 3 smoothies: 36 blackberries, 31 gooseberries. For 12 smoothies she needs ☐ berries.

7. For 4 smoothies: 44 blackberries, 53 blueberries. For 16 smoothies she needs ☐ berries.

8. For 3 smoothies: 28 blackberries, 36 raspberries. For 18 smoothies she needs ☐ berries.

Today I scored ☐ out of 8.

Week 10 — Day 1

The mirror line is shown by a dashed blue line. Reflect the shape in the mirror line. Write the coordinates of the reflection of point A.

(5, 2)

1 (,)

2 (,)

3 (,)

4 (,)

5 (,)

6 (,)

Today I scored ☐ out of 6.

Week 10 — Day 2

Work out the answer to the calculation.

623 449 − 142 527 = ?

1) 24 307 + 22 595 = ?

2) 87 458 − 25 314 = ?

3) 771 337 + 162 921 = ?

4) 344 665 − 231 438 = ?

5) 679 238 + 27 452 = ?

6) 842 109 + 31 044 =

7) 237 344 − 172 452 = ?

8) 390 237 − 27 624 = ?

Today I scored ☐ out of 8.

Week 10 — Day 3

Write down the total amount of time spent at the holiday club.

Julia goes to dance club for $2\frac{1}{4}$ hours every day for 5 days.

11 hours 15 mins

1 Zuri goes to judo club for $1\frac{1}{2}$ hours every day for 3 days.

☐ hours ☐ mins

2 Haru goes to chess club for 3 hours 20 minutes every day for 4 days.

☐ hours ☐ mins

3 Molly goes to film club for 50 minutes every day for 7 days.

☐ hours ☐ mins

4 Seb goes to craft club for $3\frac{3}{4}$ hours every day for 6 days.

☐ hours ☐ mins

5 Dilip goes to drama club for 5 hours 40 minutes every day for 5 days.

☐ hours ☐ mins

6 Phil goes to cookery club for $4\frac{1}{4}$ hours every day for 10 days.

☐ hours ☐ mins

7 Flo goes to gardening club for 6 hours 25 minutes every day for 4 days.

☐ hours ☐ mins

8 Cory goes to athletics club for 3 hours 35 minutes every day for 5 days.

☐ hours ☐ mins

Today I scored ☐ out of 8.

Year 5 Maths — Summer Term © CGP — Not to be photocopied

Week 10 — Day 4

Change the fraction into a percentage to complete the sentence. $\frac{3}{25}$ of Lucy's cows are brown. This is equal to 12%.

1. $\frac{1}{2}$ of Aysha's dogs are sausage dogs. This is equal to ___%.

2. $\frac{1}{4}$ of Matei's guinea pigs are tufty. This is equal to ___%.

3. $\frac{3}{10}$ of Joe's pigs are spotted. This is equal to ___%.

4. $\frac{7}{10}$ of Caleb's ducks are female. This is equal to ___%.

5. $\frac{1}{5}$ of Femi's hamsters escaped. This is equal to ___%.

6. $\frac{1}{25}$ of Benji's horses are named Ace. This is equal to ___%.

7. $\frac{2}{5}$ of Ayo's alpacas are white. This is equal to ___%.

8. $\frac{4}{5}$ of Kate's cats cause chaos. This is equal to ___%.

9. $\frac{4}{25}$ of Raj's fish are tropical. This is equal to ___%.

10. $\frac{7}{25}$ of Fiona's sheep are black. This is equal to ___%.

11. $\frac{9}{25}$ of Mo's rabbits have floppy ears. This is equal to ___%.

12. $\frac{21}{25}$ of Tia's parrots can talk. This is equal to ___%.

Today I scored ___ out of 12.

Week 10 — Day 5

Fill in the missing number. If 3500 beads make 70 necklaces, then 2500 beads make **50** necklaces.

1) If 400 beads make 20 necklaces, then 600 beads make ☐ necklaces.

2) If 600 jewels make 200 rings, then 1800 jewels make ☐ rings.

3) If 3000 beads make 60 bangles, then 3500 beads make ☐ bangles.

4) If 1500 jewels make 500 earrings, then 900 jewels make ☐ earrings.

5) If 2200 jewels make 200 anklets, then 3300 jewels make ☐ anklets.

6) If 3200 jewels make 40 tiaras, then 6400 jewels make ☐ tiaras.

7) If 5400 jewels make 600 rings, then 3600 jewels make ☐ rings.

8) If 4800 beads make 400 bangles, then 6000 beads make ☐ bangles.

9) If 2400 jewels make 60 tiaras, then 1600 jewels make ☐ tiaras.

10) If 2100 beads make 30 anklets, then 3500 beads make ☐ anklets.

Today I scored ☐ out of 10.

Year 5 Maths — Summer Term

Week 11 — Day 1

Kayleigh and Jamal are measuring insects. Work out the total length.

2 inches = 5 cm

Kayleigh finds a fly that measures 0.7 cm. Jamal finds an earwig that measures 2 inches. What is the total length of the insects in cm?

5.7 cm

1. Kayleigh finds a ladybird that measures 0.44 cm. Jamal finds a worm that measures 4 inches. What is the total length of the insects in cm?

   ☐ cm

2. Kayleigh finds a spider that measures 10 cm. Jamal finds a butterfly that measures 1.8 inches. What is the total length of the insects in inches?

   ☐ inches

3. Kayleigh finds a beetle that measures 3.32 cm. Jamal finds a stick insect that measures 10 inches. What is the total length of the insects in cm?

   ☐ cm

4. Kayleigh finds a cricket that measures 2.5 cm. Jamal finds a moth that measures 0.4 inches. What is the total length of the insects in inches?

   ☐ inches

5. Kayleigh finds an ant that measures 0.075 cm. Jamal finds a grasshopper that measures 1 inch. What is the total length of the insects in cm?

   ☐ cm

6. Kayleigh finds a woodlouse that measures 0.5 cm. Jamal finds a centipede that measures 1.2 inches. What is the total length of the insects in inches?

   ☐ inches

Today I scored ☐ out of 6.

Week 11 — Day 2

Work out the size of angle A in the diagram. The diagrams on this page are not drawn to scale.

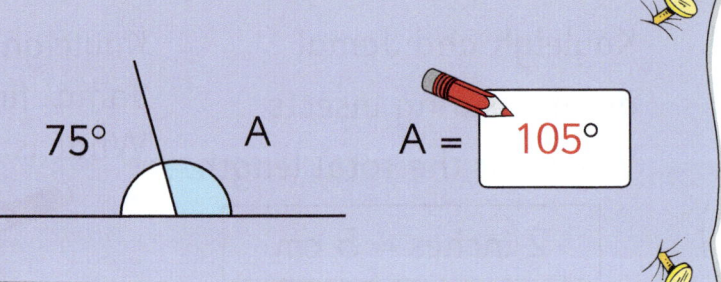

A = 105°

1) 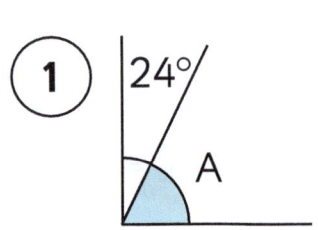 A = ___°

2) A = ___°

3) 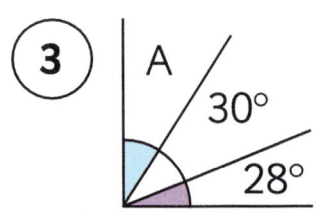 A = ___°

4) A = ___°

5) 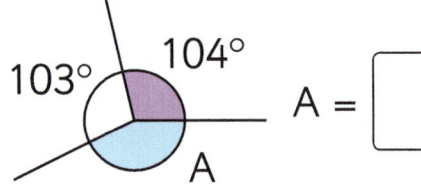 A = ___°

6) A = ___°

7) 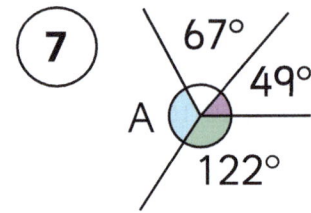 A = ___°

8) 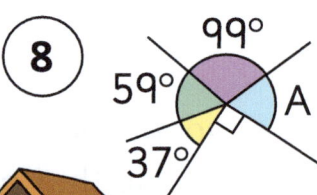 A = ___°

Today I scored ___ out of 8.

Week 11 — Day 3

1 m³ of water costs £3.20. How much would it cost to fill the swimming pool? Each cube is 1 m³.

£51.20

1. £

2. £

3. £

4. £

5. £

6. £

7. £

8. £

Today I scored ☐ out of 8.

Week 11 — Day 4

Work out the calculation. Give your answer as a mixed number.

$3\frac{3}{4} - 1\frac{1}{2} = \boxed{2\frac{1}{4}}$

1. $2\frac{1}{3} + 2\frac{1}{3} =$ ☐

2. $1\frac{4}{5} - \frac{3}{5} =$ ☐

3. $4\frac{5}{6} + 1\frac{2}{3} =$ ☐

4. $4\frac{1}{4} - 2\frac{3}{4} =$ ☐

5. $\frac{2}{9} + 1\frac{1}{3} =$ ☐

6. $5\frac{4}{12} + 5\frac{5}{6} =$ ☐

7. $9\frac{2}{9} - 6\frac{1}{3} =$ ☐

8. $2\frac{7}{8} + 4\frac{1}{2} =$ ☐

9. $6\frac{3}{4} - 5\frac{5}{12} =$ ☐

10. $3\frac{4}{5} + 2\frac{7}{15} =$ ☐

Today I scored ☐ out of 10.

Week 11 — Day 5

Work out how many items were sold in total.

A website has 500 TVs available to buy each day.
On the first day, $\frac{1}{5}$ of the TVs were sold.
On the second day, $\frac{3}{10}$ of the TVs were sold.
How many TVs were sold in total?

250

(1) A website has 100 laptops available to buy each day.
On the first day, $\frac{3}{4}$ of the laptops were sold.
On the second day, $\frac{1}{2}$ of the laptops were sold.
How many laptops were sold in total?

(2) A website has 250 kettles available to buy each day.
On the first day, $\frac{2}{5}$ of the kettles were sold.
On the second day, $\frac{3}{10}$ of the kettles were sold.
How many kettles were sold in total?

(3) A website has 200 phones available to buy each day.
On the first day, $\frac{1}{8}$ of the phones were sold.
On the second day, $\frac{5}{8}$ of the phones were sold.
How many phones were sold in total?

(4) A website has 144 lamps available to buy each day.
On the first day, $\frac{5}{6}$ of the lamps were sold.
On the second day, $\frac{5}{12}$ of the lamps were sold.
How many lamps were sold in total?

Today I scored ☐ out of 4.

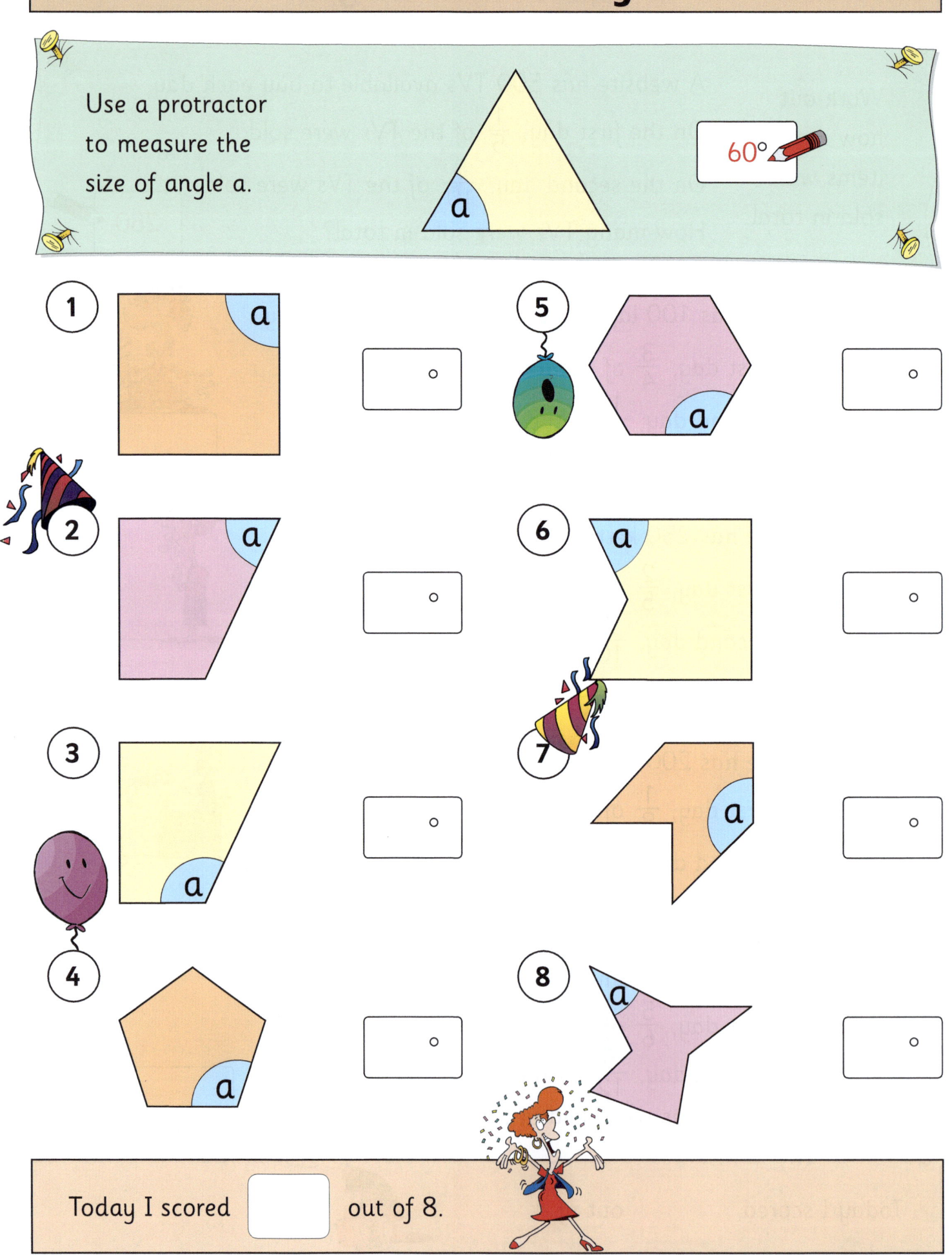

Week 12 — Day 2

Find the perimeter of the rectangle. The rectangles are not drawn to scale.

22.65 m, 7.823 m → **60.946 m**

1. 20.10 m, 4.205 m
2. 37.12 m, 4.144 m
3. 21.51 m, 5.925 m
4. 18.91 m, 6.603 m
5. 32.26 m, 7.028 m
6. 35.68 m, 8.367 m
7. 39.34 m, 7.891 m
8. 42.77 m, 6.974 m
9. 28.97 m, 9.719 m
10. 45.84 m, 8.849 m

Today I scored ____ out of 10.

Week 12 — Day 3

Work out the answer to the calculation.   6524 ÷ 7 = 932

1) 3212 × 12 =

2) 7648 ÷ 4 =

3) 2156 × 17 =

4) 8103 ÷ 3 =

5) 5163 × 25 =

6) 7285 ÷ 5 =

7) 3932 × 31 =

8) 5988 ÷ 6 =

9) 9744 × 29 =

10) 7074 ÷ 9 =

Today I scored ☐ out of 10.

Week 12 — Day 4

Circle the total fraction of the shape that is shaded.

1.  $\frac{40}{80}$ $\frac{3}{4}$ $\frac{10}{16}$

5. 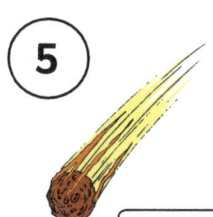  $\frac{7}{8}$ $\frac{35}{88}$ $\frac{21}{48}$

2.  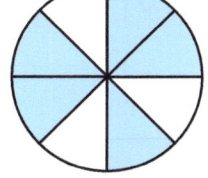 $\frac{15}{20}$ $\frac{13}{24}$ $\frac{25}{40}$

6.  $\frac{18}{40}$ $\frac{32}{80}$ $\frac{11}{30}$

3. 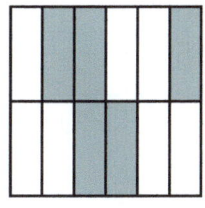 $\frac{15}{36}$ $\frac{2}{6}$ $\frac{45}{60}$

7.  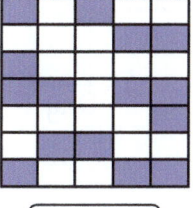 $\frac{35}{70}$ $\frac{20}{35}$ $\frac{3}{7}$

4.  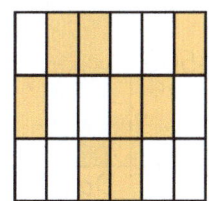 $\frac{25}{54}$ $\frac{18}{36}$ $\frac{4}{9}$

8.  $\frac{49}{84}$ $\frac{10}{21}$ $\frac{2}{3}$

Today I scored 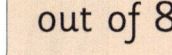 out of 8.

© CGP — Not to be photocopied

Year 5 Maths — Summer Term

Week 12 — Day 5

15 000 people visited a theme park over 4 days. The graph shows how many visitors rode one of the rides each day. How many visitors did not ride the ride?

2500

1.

2.

3.

4.

5.

6.

Today I scored ☐ out of 6.

Answers

Week 1 — Day 1
For Q1-8 below, allow any answer in the range given.
1. 73-77°
2. 18-22°
3. 65-69°
4. 134-138°
5. 160-164°
6. 146-150°
7. 24-28°
8. 121-125°

Week 1 — Day 2
1. three hundred and forty eight thousand, five hundred and twenty nine
2. two hundred and sixty four thousand and eighty seven
3. nine hundred and fifty six thousand, eight hundred and twenty three
4. eight hundred and eighty thousand, two hundred and forty four
5. three hundred and six thousand, five hundred and two
6. one million, four hundred and seventy three thousand and one
7. six million, nine hundred and two thousand, six hundred
8. three million, sixty seven thousand, eight hundred and nine

Week 1 — Day 3
1. 27
2. 36
3. 135
4. 138
5. 56
6. 77
7. 264
8. 336

Week 1 — Day 4
1. 975 ml
2. 420 ml
3. 1.12 l
4. 350 ml
5. 3 l
6. 4.29 l
7. 2.42 l
8. 2.72 l

Week 1 — Day 5
1. 25 km
2. 25 km
3. 60 km
4. 28 km
5. 33 km
6. 36 km
7. 36 km
8. 29 km

Week 2 — Day 1
1. 4221
2. 6875
3. 2519
4. 98 662
5. 44 899
6. 55 647
7. 83 231
8. 69 899

Week 2 — Day 2
1. 5 cm
2. 6.6 cm
3. 22 cm
4. 4.4 cm
5. 9.9 cm

Week 2 — Day 3
1. $5\frac{1}{3}$
2. $22\frac{1}{2}$
3. 12
4. $13\frac{1}{2}$ or $13\frac{2}{4}$
5. $30\frac{3}{5}$
6. $7\frac{1}{2}$ or $7\frac{3}{6}$

Week 2 — Day 4
1. 2000
2. 2007
3. 1901
4. 1700
5. 2045
6. 1240
7. 1980
8. 1822
9. 978
10. 1334
11. 852
12. 1869

Week 2 — Day 5
1. 108 kg
2. 3 kg
3. 128 kg
4. 330 kg
5. 5.6 kg
6. 1392 kg
7. 6.615 kg
8. 357.6 kg

Week 3 — Day 1
1. 3 m
2. 6 m
3. 72 feet
4. 114 feet
5. 36 m
6. 2850 feet
7. 0.5 m
8. 10.5 feet
9. 4.5 m
10. 31.5 feet
11. 85.5 feet
12. 57 m

Week 3 — Day 2
1. 2, 5
2. 11, 7
3. 2, 5
4. 3, 11
5. 2, 7, 3
6. 2, 13
7. 5, 3, 2

Week 3 — Day 3
1. 11:49
2. 20:15
3. 14:01
4. 17:48
5. 06:36
6. 23:18
7. 23:49
8. 00:10

Week 3 — Day 4
1. 32
2. 2
3. 3
4. 12
5. 12
6. 63

Week 3 — Day 5
1. 2
2. 18
3. 13
4. 9
5. 7
6. 7
7. 4
8. 10

Week 4 — Day 1
1. 19, 14, 9, 4
2. 11, 5, −1, −7
3. 36, 21, 6, −9
4. 21, 10, −1, −12
5. 61, 39, 17, −5
6. 40, 21, 2, −17
7. 154, 100, 46, −8
8. 127, 84, 41, −2

Week 4 — Day 2
1. 67°
2. 41°
3. 105°
4. 27°
5. 16°
6. 20°
7. 68°
8. 52°
9. 58°
10. 127°
11. 125°
12. 67°

Week 4 — Day 3
1. 6734
2. 5927
3. 3684
4. 2421
5. 1581
6. 1562
7. 519
8. 59

Week 4 — Day 4
1. 4
2. 9
3. 36
4. 16
5. 1
6. 49
7. 64
8. 100
9. 81
10. 121

Week 4 — Day 5
1. 2 × 2 × 2
2. 8 × 8
3. 1
4. 49
5. 9 + 4
6. 5 × 25
7. 81
8. 64 − 1

Week 5 — Day 1
1. Saturday
2. Monday
3. Tuesday
4. Tuesday
5. Wednesday
6. Friday
7. Wednesday
8. Saturday

Week 5 — Day 2
1. 147
2. 32
3. 64
4. 8
5. 5
6. 8
7. 128
8. 3
9. 2
10. 7
11. 3
12. 2

Week 5 — Day 3
1. 4 in
2. 60 cm
3. 48 in
4. 300 cm
5. 60 in
6. 90 cm
7. 16 in
8. 45 cm
9. 30 in
10. 135 cm
11. 80 in
12. 50 cm

Week 5 — Day 4
1. $\frac{1}{4}, \frac{5}{8}, \frac{3}{4}, \frac{7}{8}$
2. $\frac{1}{6}, \frac{1}{3}, \frac{2}{3}, \frac{5}{6}$
3. $\frac{1}{12}, \frac{5}{12}, \frac{17}{24}, \frac{5}{6}$
4. $\frac{5}{18}, \frac{7}{18}, \frac{16}{36}, \frac{7}{9}$
5. $\frac{1}{4}, \frac{3}{8}, \frac{1}{2}, \frac{10}{16}$
6. $\frac{6}{40}, \frac{13}{20}, \frac{7}{10}, \frac{4}{5}$
7. $\frac{33}{100}, \frac{17}{50}, \frac{7}{10}, \frac{47}{50}$
8. $\frac{3}{28}, \frac{16}{56}, \frac{5}{14}, \frac{5}{7}$

Week 5 — Day 5
1. 3000
2. 4000
3. 3000
4. 20 000
5. 15 000
6. 105 000

Week 6 — Day 1
1. 42 cm²
2. 24 cm²
3. 99 cm²
4. 60 cm²
5. 40 cm²
6. 39 cm²
7. 84 cm²
8. 60 cm²
9. 84 cm²
10. 51 cm²
11. 104 cm²
12. 80 cm²

Week 6 — Day 2
1. 6052
2. 18 798
3. 145 132
4. 30 264
5. 148 771
6. 217 005
7. 556 702
8. 403 008

Week 6 — Day 3
1. 100
2. 600
3. 750
4. 600
5. 180
6. 270

Week 6 — Day 4
1. 1.7 m
2. 2.8 kg
3. 5 km
4. 4200 m
5. 3.6 litres
6. 125 cm
7. 9100 g
8. 10 000 ml
9. 4.32 m
10. 1.15 kg
11. 2610 m
12. 7.3 litres

Week 6 — Day 5
1. 1982
2. 1427
3. 2644
4. 2341
5. 1769
6. 2199
7. 2489
8. 2748

Week 7 — Day 1

1. $\frac{1}{10}, \frac{100}{1000}, \frac{10}{100}$
2. $\frac{400}{1000}, \frac{4}{10}, \frac{40}{100}$
3. $\frac{600}{1000}, \frac{60}{100}$
4. $\frac{1}{2}, \frac{500}{1000}, \frac{50}{100}$
5. $\frac{2}{10}, \frac{1}{5}, \frac{200}{1000}$
6. $\frac{800}{1000}, \frac{40}{50}$
7. $\frac{22}{20}, \frac{11}{10}, \frac{1100}{1000}$
8. $\frac{90}{100}, \frac{900}{1000}$
9. $\frac{15}{10}, \frac{1500}{1000}$
10. $\frac{240}{200}, \frac{6}{5}, \frac{1200}{1000}$

Week 7 — Day 2

1.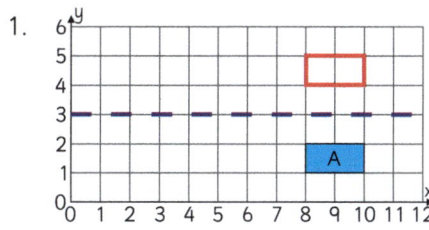
2.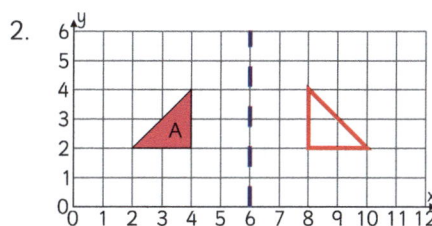
3.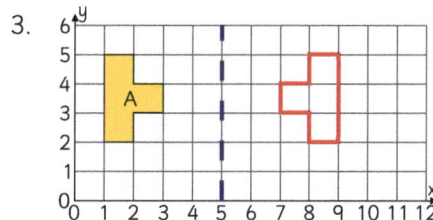
4.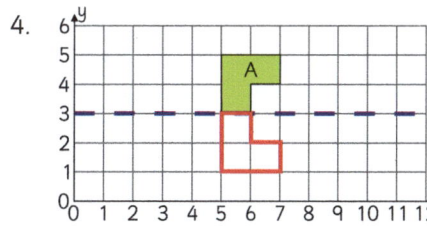
5.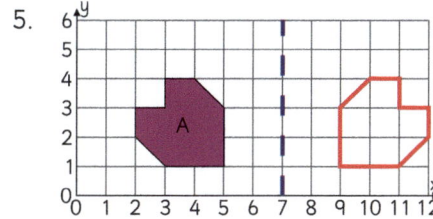

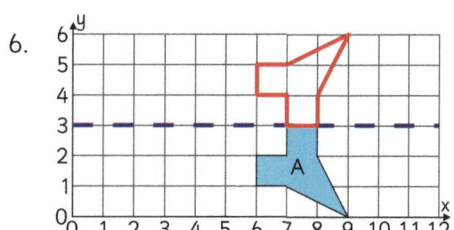

Week 7 — Day 3

1. 0.123
2. 0.47
3. 0.698
4. 0.902
5. 1.084
6. 1.205
7. 1.98
8. 0.092
9. 3.419
10. 0.04
11. 6.001
12. 7.068

Week 7 — Day 4

1. Shape A to B: 2 down
   Shape A to C: 8 right
2. Shape A to B: 3 left
   Shape A to C: 3 left and 3 up
3. Shape A to B: 4 left and 1 down
   Shape A to C: 9 left and 2 down
4. Shape A to B: 3 left and 2 up
   Shape A to C: 4 right and 3 up

Week 7 — Day 5

1. coffee
2. lemon
3. raspberry
4. walnut
5. lemon
6. strawberry

Week 8 — Day 1

1. 2.077
2. 5.991
3. 4.382
4. 3.081
5. 7.758
6. 1.429
7. 9.306
8. 6.244
9. 1.973
10. 2.865
11. 4.541
12. 8.881

Week 8 — Day 2

1. 5.851 m
2. 3.972 m
3. 4.708 m
4. 5.893 m
5. 5.098 m
6. 6.492 m
7. 6.617 m
8. 8.009 m

Week 8 — Day 3

1. 76 minutes
2. 66 minutes
3. 35 minutes
4. 79 minutes
5. 94 minutes
6. 114 minutes

Week 8 — Day 4

1. 280 ml
2. 31
3. 2.1 m
4. 18
5. 42
6. 13
7. 224 g
8. 84

Week 8 — Day 5

1. 84 cm
2. 100 cm
3. 64 cm
4. 128 cm
5. 84 cm
6. 136 cm

Week 9 — Day 1

1. 12% — 0.12
   35% — 0.35
   66% — 0.66
2. 27% — 0.27
   10% — 0.1
   81% — 0.81
3. 52% — 0.52
   5% — 0.05
   20% — 0.2
4. 93% — 0.93
   80% — 0.8
   9% — 0.09

Week 9 — Day 2

1. acute
2. obtuse
3. acute
4. reflex
5. obtuse
6. reflex
7. acute
8. obtuse
9. obtuse
10. reflex
11. reflex
12. obtuse

Week 9 — Day 3

1. 25%
2. £33
3. £2
4. 70%
5. 20%
6. 4%
7. £120
8. £22
9. 78%
10. £43

Week 9 — Day 4

1. 15%
2. 0.45
3. 10%
4. 0.29
5. 58%
6. 89%
7. $\frac{1}{2}$
8. 72%
9. 0.21
10. $\frac{35}{50}$
11. 0.57
12. 3%

Week 9 — Day 5

1. 230
2. 180
3. 279
4. 217
5. 198
6. 268
7. 388
8. 384

Week 10 — Day 1

1. 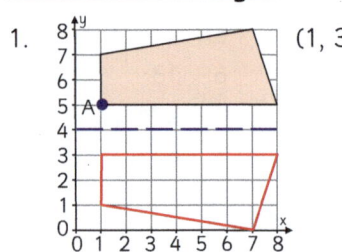 (1, 3)
2. 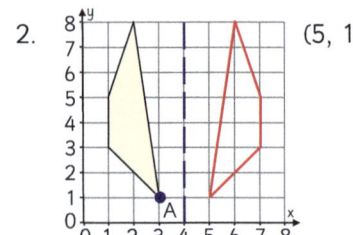 (5, 1)
3. 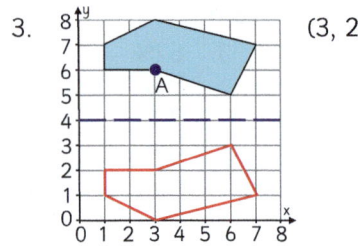 (3, 2)
4. 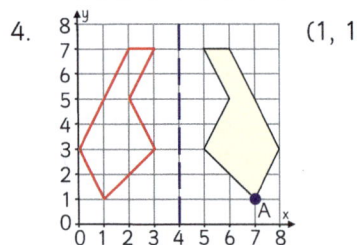 (1, 1)
5. 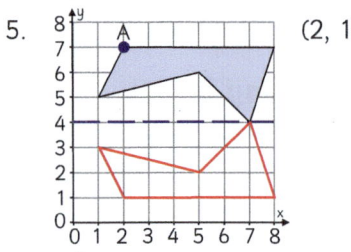 (2, 1)
6. 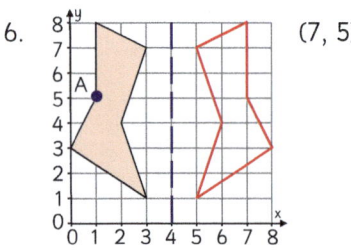 (7, 5)

Week 10 — Day 2

1. 46 902
2. 62 144
3. 934 258
4. 113 227
5. 706 690
6. 873 153
7. 64 892
8. 362 613

Week 10 — Day 3

1. 4 hours 30 mins
2. 13 hours 20 mins
3. 5 hours 50 mins
4. 22 hours 30 mins
5. 28 hours 20 mins
6. 42 hours 30 mins
7. 25 hours 40 mins
8. 17 hours 55 mins

Week 10 — Day 4

1. 50%
2. 25%
3. 30%
4. 70%
5. 20%
6. 4%
7. 40%
8. 80%
9. 16%
10. 28%
11. 36%
12. 84%

Week 10 — Day 5

1. 30
2. 600
3. 70
4. 300
5. 300
6. 80
7. 400
8. 500
9. 40
10. 50

Week 11 — Day 1

1. 10.44 cm
2. 5.8 inches
3. 28.32 cm
4. 1.4 inches
5. 2.575 cm
6. 1.4 inches

Week 11 — Day 2

1. 66°
2. 33°
3. 32°
4. 26°
5. 153°
6. 136°
7. 122°
8. 75°

Week 11 — Day 3

1. £57.60
2. £44.80
3. £76.80
4. £153.60
5. £51.20
6. £38.40
7. £80
8. £64

Week 11 — Day 4

1. $4\frac{2}{3}$
2. $1\frac{1}{5}$
3. $6\frac{1}{2}$ or $6\frac{3}{6}$
4. $1\frac{2}{4}$ or $1\frac{1}{2}$
5. $1\frac{5}{9}$
6. $6\frac{6}{7}$ or $6\frac{12}{14}$
7. $11\frac{1}{6}$ or $11\frac{2}{12}$
8. $2\frac{8}{9}$
9. $1\frac{1}{3}$ or $1\frac{4}{12}$
10. $6\frac{4}{15}$

Week 11 — Day 5

1. 125
2. 175
3. 150
4. 180

Week 12 — Day 1

For Q1-8 below, allow any answer in the range given.

1. 88-92°
2. 63-67°
3. 113-117°
4. 106-110°
5. 118-122°
6. 63-67°
7. 133-137°
8. 35-39°

Week 12 — Day 2

1. 48.61 m
2. 82.528 m
3. 54.87 m
4. 51.026 m
5. 78.576 m
6. 88.094 m
7. 94.462 m
8. 99.488 m
9. 77.378 m
10. 109.378 m

Week 12 — Day 3

1. 38 544
2. 1912
3. 36 652
4. 2701
5. 129 075
6. 1457
7. 121 892
8. 998
9. 282 576
10. 786

Week 12 — Day 4

1. $\frac{40}{80}$
2. $\frac{25}{40}$
3. $\frac{15}{36}$
4. $\frac{4}{9}$
5. $\frac{21}{48}$
6. $\frac{32}{80}$
7. $\frac{3}{7}$
8. $\frac{10}{21}$

Week 12 — Day 5

1. 5000
2. 10 000
3. 8750
4. 5800
5. 750
6. 3300